da 'votions from da 'hood

Stories and Reflections on Experiencing Jesus while Living and Serving in the Inner-City

Jeffrey Anderson

Copyright © 2015 Jeffrey Anderson
All Rights Reserved
ISBN 978-1-312-78271-6

INTRODUCTION

Depleted. Drained. Hopeless. Utterly exhausted.

Those were some of the words friends and colleagues used to describe themselves after spending a few days serving with me in Baltimore's neighborhood known as Pigtown. Pretty much all the issues of an impoverished and crime-ridden neighborhood flourish there in broad daylight for all to witness.

Defining my role as pastor in this context was complex at best. Competing spiritual, psychological, and temporal philosophies came into play. I regularly received direction from outsiders like:

"We need more government programs to help people overcome their circumstances."

"People here should not depend on the government and instead need to develop better work ethics and money management."

"We need to isolate problems and focus our energies on solving them."

"Stop looking at all the problems and instead find the good things that are happening and help them take root."

"This place is a battleground between good and evil so you must equip people to stand strong through the Word."

"It's much more important that people understand and apply the principles of the gospel than it is to know the Biblical text."

To all those statements I say Amen.

But those opinions about things did not help clarify my roles and responsibilities as a resident and pastor of this neighborhood. How was I to live and work week after week in an environment that left people feeling depleted, drained, hopeless, and utterly exhausted after only a few days?

In this context, I found myself moving more and more into the role of witness; I observed the where, when, and how of God's work in people's lives and shared that with them and others as appropriate. But my understanding of what God was doing in someone's life was often at odds with what *they* thought was happening, especially in the heat of the moment before hindsight clarified our vision.

I came to discover that, in all honesty, the only things to which I could assuredly testify were the things I had seen God do in me. His call to repentance, a hope for what could be, or a glimpse into the spirit realm via the temporal was the tool I had to keep myself engaged in the mission of building God's kingdom in the here and now.

To help me keep track, I started jotting down brief statements to jog my memory. Of the hundreds of events I noted, a few grew into essays and stories. After trying out rough drafts on a blog and letting them sit for a few years, I collected a handful of them here for this book.

Some stories are lighthearted. Some are disturbing. All of them have shaped my understanding of the Holy and my life's response to Him.

I hope these stories help you come to know God better. Not so much because you've learned my stories, though. My hope is that they will help you better witness the Spirit's work in you each day and help you in your journey from where you are to where you are called to be.

AWESOME

Just after sunset one summer night several of us were working on a mural on the side of a building in our neighborhood. The mural featured Jesus carrying a baby, pulling a wagon full of kids with toys, and several children following after him.

While we were working, a local prostitute, obviously stung out on drugs that night, staggered briskly down the other side of the street. She paused as she hollered out at us, "That Jesus is F***ing AWESOME!" then continued on her way.

As a Christian I'm used to words such as *awesome*, *wonderful*, *majestic*, and the like to describe God. They roll off the tongue but don't always connect with the reality of awe and wonder and mystery that I so easily miss in the chaos of daily living. I get distracted by traffic and television and personal crisis and debates about what color the new carpeting at the church should be, burying the sense of awe and wonder of who God is, what Jesus has done for us, and how the Holy Spirit continues to move each day.

Perhaps this is part of why Jesus is remembered in Matthew (21:31) as having commented that people like our local prostitute could more likely get into the Kingdom before the religious types like me. This unabashed and uninhibited recognition of the awesomeness of Jesus expressed by those just barely getting by on the fringes of society is something I can easily backburner amid my supposedly important priorities and push the Kingdom just a little further away.

How can I live each day with the passion for Jesus expressed as freely and unashamedly as our local prostitute that night? Do I sometimes become so habitual with my faith that there's no room for wonder? If I realized that Jesus is even more awesome than the prostitute expressed and lived out that awesomeness in my daily activities what would my life be like? Our churches be like? Our world be like?

Jesus, fill us with awe for You. Help me to live in the wonder and mystery that You are and invite all to live in Your indescribable presence each moment.

DIGNITY

It was an exciting day when the church moved into its new building. The old building was a rat-infested smelly dilapidated fire trap of disgust (those who have been there know that this description is grossly understated) that God had used to do a great work in people's lives. The new building was clean and fresh and bright and wonderful in every way.

The first Wednesday after the grand opening the 12-step group that had been meeting for several years in the old building held its regular session at the new location. Afterward, several of the group's members asked to meet with me.

They all had concerned looks on their faces and hesitated to speak. One finally asked, "Is it really OK for us to meet in here?" Confused by the question, I answered, "Of course" with a perplexed expression on my face.

A couple of them started to tear up. Another spoke, "No, you don't understand. Most of us aren't *allowed* in nice places. We've done a lot of bad things and aren't welcome someplace nice like this. Are you sure we can really meet here each week?"

After several more assurances, they left boisterously with a new spring in their steps.

For me, much of the work the Gospel is focused on this very thing. When I can help restore dignity in others in big and small ways I am correctly answering the question "What Would Jesus Do?" I see Him touching the leper, talking with the Samaritan woman, valuing the widow's mite, and accepting the perfume poured over his head. In these and other acts, dignity was restored.

For those of us who follow Him, we can look forward to a moment similar to the one experienced by the 12-step group. He has promised to go to the Father's house to prepare a place for us (John 14:2). It's not the kind of place that we would normally be allowed to go. Yet, in that place our dignity as one created and loved by Him will be fully restored.

Lord God, as I go about my day help me to begin to restore dignity in the lives of those I meet even as You have done and continue to do in me.

PRECISION

Fifty-seven cents.

That was the balance of the church checkbook when I left the neighborhood for a few days of meetings at church headquarters. We had been through a series of expensive crises in rapid succession without a whole lot of cash to start with. Our donors from outside the neighborhood had been generous enough to keep us afloat for the past two months. With all our regular bills and summer camp fees on the horizon we were down to fifty-seven cents.

After the final service of the event at headquarters I stopped by the sanctuary for one last set of prayers before catching the plane home into the reality of the world of fifty-seven cents.

In the silence just before I whispered an "Amen," a woman sat down in the pew behind me, leaned up and whispered in my ear, "You're Jeff from Baltimore, right?" Upon my nod, she said, "Take this" and darted out of the room.

What she had stuffed in my hand was a few bills – a couple 20s, a 5, some 1s – *exactly* enough cash to buy the pizzas for the evening's youth activities that I was to lead upon landing. The kids' daily bread with tomato sauce and cheese on top had just been provided with fifty-seven cents to spare.

All the problems were not solved and the systemic financial crisis was not over, but things were OK. They were OK because of the precision of God's understanding of the situation.

Yes, He could have followed my plan by sending $1M, taking the full temporal burden away. But the reminder of His intimate understanding of the needs at hand carried me further than my quick fix idea would have.

Jesus reminds us that even the hairs on our heads are numbered (Luke 12:7). Even when going bald (in my case sometimes figuratively, always literally), the knowledge that He knows me and my situation with immeasurable precision makes me a little more willing to let Him work in His ways rather than trying to force my ways on Him.

Lord, help me always to remember how well You know me and my circumstances. Through that knowledge let me better trust Your ways in my life.

FIGHT

As the last of the kids were leaving their Sunday afternoon activities at the church, two of our faithful participants started a full-on fist fight blocking the exit door.

It was not an even match. One kid was a short, spindly 8 year old while the other was an 11 year old who looked like a linebacker. We separated the boys and held their adrenaline-filled bodies far enough apart to let the rest of the group exit.

Hoping to invoke the peacemaking skills she'd been teaching in recent lessons, one of our volunteers stood between them and in her best Sunday-school-teacher voice calmly asked, "What would Jesus do?"

The older boy raised his hand and She gently acknowledged him. He passionately replied, "He would tell that little boy to get down on his knees and repent!" Hearing that, the little one dashed out the door and down the street. The other made chase. After hitting each other for a few minutes they were OK with being friends again and walked down the street together.

Somewhere in my brain is an image of God calling me to repentance and my immediate, respectful bowing at His throne in submission. The reality of the relationship, though, is a series of me squabbling with

Him followed by my running down the street trying to escape.

I'm really glad that in Genesis 32 Jacob's name was changed to Israel and that his descendants, as God's people, were called Israelites. Loosely translated, the word Israel means *one who wrestles with God*. It reminds me that the ones who are willing to really wrestle with Him are the ones who will be called His people.

The One who is bigger than me continues to call me to repentance. When I get tired of running I will cry *Why God Why?* and *When God When?* and *You want me to do WHAT?!?* as we take it to the mat. I know He will win, but the wrestling both wears down my resistance and builds up my strength.

Once we wrestle a bit, I'm OK being friends again. It's then that I can resume my walk down the road with Him.

Lord, help me each day to be repentant and not be afraid of being one You would name Israel. Let my struggles with You take me to where I might become more fully Yours.

WHY

The President of the church surprised us with a visit. We knew he was in the area for another event and we learned at the last minute he would be able to stop by for our kids' activities on Sunday afternoon and for our evening services later that day.

He arrived just as the kids gathered. They had no idea who he was or why he was there.

After we sang our songs and offered prayer, we turned the lesson time over to the President so he could talk with the kids. After asking them some questions about who they were, he asked, "Why do you come here?"

This was when I panicked.

My immediate silent prayer was, "Good Lord don't let them answer 'Because we get candy bars after the lesson'!"

Hands shot up immediately and he called on the boy I thought most likely to give a full description of the types of candy he preferred. The boy answered, "To be in the presence of God." The next kid answered, "To learn things from the Bible." The one after that said, "So I can practice how God wants me to live each day." The fourth said, "Because it's peaceful here."

I have to admit that I often go to church just for the candy bars. I like being around people I know, singing the songs I like, hearing from my favorite scripture passages, and sharing in testimonies about how God has been nice to those who have gathered.

I want to be more able to answer as the kids did:

-*To be in the presence of God* knowing that His presence is wonderful yet carries conviction that loves me so much it scares me enough to correct what isn't right and to do things I don't want to do.

-*To learn things from the Bible* knowing that if I look more closely at my favorite passages I realize that I've only scratched the surface of their meaning and that the pages that are less familiar are filled with issues, concepts, and Truth that are hard for me to understand, much less embrace.

-*So I can practice how God wants me to live each day* knowing that it means that I need to go deep into the messiness of other people's lives and let other people go deep into my own mess so that together we can practice patients, kindness, mercy, grace, compassion, faithfulness, endurance, acceptance, correction, love.

-*Because it's peaceful here* knowing that peace is rooted both in the choice God makes to live at peace with me despite myself and in my call to share that peace with others despite *them*selves and *my*self.

Candy bars are delicious. But a diet heavy in them, no matter how tasty, leaves me flabby and starved. The kids said they came to church for the meat and potatoes of the Gospel along with the Fruit of the Spirit. May I be able to honestly answer something better than "because of the candy bars" the next time someone asks me why I go to church.

Lord, nourish me at your banquet. Guide my cravings to the spiritual foods that will help me grow strong in You.

NEED

As people were gathering before the Sunday morning service, a woman who lived across the street from the church whipped open the door and ran across the back of the room at full speed. One second later she dashed back out of the building, plunger in hand.

Just a few minutes after that and still in time for church, she returned at a more relaxed pace and put the plunger back in the women's restroom.

To those of us still chuckling and with inquisitive looks on our faces, she announced, "I thought I was headed for a disaster. But then I remembered that what I needed was here in the church."

When we think we're headed for disaster do we remember that what we really need is in the Church? No, the church can't immediately solve all of our problems for us.

But when the Church is alive, in it are encouragement, wisdom, truth, support, correction, help, comfort, healing and strength.

In it is the reminder that we are not alone, both because of the presence of his Spirit and the presence of His people.

In it our impending disasters are not measured by the world's standards but by the power God gives us to endure, to overcome, and to become more than conquerors.

Can the Church become known in the world as the place that, when disaster seems imminent, people can find what they really need?

Joy. Hope. Love. Peace. Community.

And, occasionally, a plunger.

Lord, help me to genuinely be a part of the Church. Help me bring what is truly needed into the lives of all those I encounter this day.

PEACE

The Peacemobile came to town! We hosted this traveling exhibit of interactive activity centers at the church as the children from the nearby elementary school came in, two or three classes at a time, to learn about how they can have personal peace, interpersonal peace, cross-cultural peace, and environmental peace.

One of the kids in a group I took through the activity centers lived on my street. She was completely engaged in each of the activities and took a leadership role in the group. In debriefing at the end of each activity she had a solid concept of peace and some skills in building it.

That evening I could hear echoing up the street the adult in her life scream profanity at her and then hear her painful cries as her body was struck repeatedly throughout the evening.

Did 45 minutes with some activities at the church make her life any better? I don't know. I do know, though, that despite what happened later in the day, she experienced 45 minutes of peace that morning.

You and I meet a lot of people each day. We have no ideas what battles they're in the midst of fighting for their physical, psychological, emotional, and spiritual survival. If we really knew what was happening in the lives our cashier, coworker, supervisor, teacher, waiter, or neighbor who lives across the street we would probably be overwhelmed.

This only amplifies the need for me to be a Peacemobile in my world. A lot of days I am more like a tank crashing through everything and everyone. But if I can lower the guns and harmonize with the world around me, reach across cultural barriers, try to get along with others, and respect myself enough to actually live the ways of peace I might, might, might, might, might provide someone a few moments of respite from the battles that engulf them.

Jesus said, "Come to me and I will give you rest." (Matthew 11:28b) Can we be that place of rest for those we encounter in a war-torn world?

Lord, make me a channel of your peace;
where there is hatred, let me sow love;
where there is injury, your pardon Lord;
and where there's doubt, true faith in you.
                              --- St. Francis

CALL

It was love at first sight.

A friend of mine was in town for a few days to get some ideas to use in her ministry. Then he walked in. Their eyes met. Instantly he knew. He was about 12 years old and it was as if he'd met his long lost grandmother.

He was at church more that weekend than any other time I can remember. He would come early and stay late just to be around her a little more. Between activities he would run down the block to his house to "put on something nice," something we'd never seen him do before.

And the feeling was mutual. This kid had instantly gotten into my friends heart. Between activities she would ask more details about his life. She gave him lots of special attention throughout the weekend. He was clearly her favorite.

After the final activity on Sunday evening she and I were debriefing her visit. Naturally, she asked some more questions about this boy. Somehow it came up that he had not been baptized

A kind of panic came over her. She emphatically declared, "I've got to find him." She dashed out onto our dark street that dark September night and started yelling his name. Over and over again she called in desperation as her voice echoed off the row houses. She had to see him one more time.

After a few minutes he came out of his house. They had a long, quiet, private conversation on the sidewalk directly in front of the church then parted. Relieved, she came back into the church to continue with our conversation.

How strange and wonderful it must have been for him to be in his house and to recognize his name being called out. How strange and wonderful it is when we hear the One who loves us calling our name.

Have you heard your name called out by the One who loves you? Over and over and over His voice echoes through all of creation calling us to step out from where we are and to come to Him.

He's been in love with us since the beginning of time. Though we have a long history of doing all we can to ignore the calling, to reject the love, to hide and keep our distance, to try to be unlovable, He still calls out to us day and night.

I shudder to think of the distress my friend would have experienced had the boy not come back outside that night. To what lengths would she have been willing and able to go between that moment and her flight home the next day in order to let him know how much he is loved? And none of us knew on that night of September 9, 2001, how much we would need to cling to Love's foundation in just a few short hours.

Listen. Your name is echoing down the streets. Your Creator calls you by your name. He wants you to know even more of His love. He wants to encourage, equip, and empower you to live in His love each moment. Step out your door and come to the sound of His voice.

Lord, let me hear Your love's call. Let me respond in love to that call and come out of my world to You.

UNDERESTIMATE

To say I was hesitant to teach about finances, especially tithing, in the middle of a neighborhood known as having the 7th highest concentration of urban poverty in the US was an understatement. I had decided outright not to do it.

Initially, this was fine. Many "ministers" had scammed people in the area over the years and when I arrived the already established policy at the church was to not ask for money from those who gathered. This was healthy, appropriate, and good.

WAS.

I had a growing conviction that the season for hesitation was over and that I needed to teach people to give. I was not interested in doing so. For over a year I wrestled with God, argued with my conscience, and all but printed out charts and graphs to justify my mind's decision.

The Spirit wasn't all that interested in my thoughts and feelings on the subject.

I finally stood before the congregation and told them that I had to confess before them. THAT got their attention! I told them of my wrestling with a topic I needed to teach but didn't want to. I apologized and told them that the day's sermon topic was on money.

At that point, everyone ---- EVERYONE ---- perked up. The group that had gathered that day was riveted as I talked about tithing and first fruits and savings and the responsibilities that come with material positions.

The real shocker for me came the next Sunday. After that service I opened the little offering box and it had more than just the usual few dollars in it. It was nowhere near our expenses for the week but it was a seven-fold increase over the previous week.

I didn't know how to feel: Happy that people had responded? Guilty wondering if people were going hungry because of it? Humbled at the sacrifice? Encouraged by the sense of ownership people displayed? Thankful for the bounty?

The Spirit said, "Peace."

The Sunday after that, the amount given doubled again. Two families in the congregation privately pulled me aside and told me that they had committed themselves to tithe.

Now, I'm not a prosperity preacher; I don't believe that that size of your faith determines the size of your Cadillac. But it seems that whenever we step out in faith the Spirit blesses us in wonderful and mysterious ways. And within two months of those families having followed the Spirit's conviction and faithfully committed to tithing, each were given a car. These gifts were unsolicited, didn't come from people in church, and were complete surprises.

And I didn't know how to feel then, either. I think the reason for that is the same reason I wrestled with teaching about money in the first place.

That reason is my tendency to underestimate God. It comes out of my own foolishness and faithlessness. We read in Isaiah 55:8 (NIV) "For my thoughts are not your thoughts, neither are your ways my ways," declares the LORD." Because His ways are (thankfully!) so different from mine I can't predict what He will do or how He will do it.

I guess that's where faith comes in. It took faith from a variety of people to let this story come to light. Faith to follow the Spirit to teach an uncomfortable subject. Faith to tithe. Faith to recognize the source of the blessing. Faith to credit the Spirit's movement despite underestimating what He will do.

Lord, as I journey with You help me to look beyond what I can see, trusting in Your ways and never underestimating what You might do.

SIN

The young cousin of the guy who was in charge of all the drug deals in our neighborhood moved in with him for a few months. The church was just down the street from their house and when the church doors were open this kid was inside.

Not long after he arrived, he handed me a couple of loose-leaf pages he had decorated. I opened them to see his art work. Along with the drawings of the church building and some illustration of the activities there was the statement "Be a Sin."

On the second page he wrote an acrostic of how to "Be a Sin":

B - Behave yourself
E - Easy on Bad News

A - Act in a Proper Way

S - Survive through the Bad Things
I - Intelligent --- Show your act
N - be Nice to Grown Ups

Needless to say, I was curious as to where he came up with this idea. He said, "Well, sin is a word I've heard at some of the churches I've been to so I figured it must be something people who go to church are supposed to be."

I have to wonder how many people have gotten confused about things because people at church are busy "Being a Sin."

I don't mean this in the way the described in the acrostic. I mean that sometimes as a Christian I display the exact opposite of what I'm trying to teach. It's so easy to do.

It's so easy when I receive insight and wisdom to be a sin and live in arrogance rather than in humility.

It's so easy when I receive material blessings to be a sin and live in greed rather than in generosity and abundance.

It's so easy when I feel supported and loved in a community's fellowship to be a sin and exclude others who are desperately seeking it

It's so easy when I have been delivered from my destructive habits to be a sin and condemn those who are still ensnared.

It's so easy when I have a place of sanctuary to be a sin and withdraw from the world rather than to engage it.

Isn't the church often portrayed in the media as arrogant, greedy, exclusive, condemning, and withdrawn? Sometimes my own "Being a Sin" is what has helped that image have a bit of truth in it.

If I'm going to be accused of "Being a Sin," then I want to be the kind of "sin" that our neighbor boy described: behaving myself, easy on the bad news, acting in a proper way, surviving through the bad things, intelligent and showing my act, and nice to grown-ups.

Like the kid said, it's how ". . . people who go to church are supposed to be."

Lord, forgive me when I've abandoned Your ways amid Your blessings. Let my actions and attitudes reflect Your light and, in doing so, let your Way live in me.

SENSELESSNESS

She got home just before dawn after completing her night shift on the cleaning staff at the university. She stepped into her 14 year old daughter's room to check on her. What she found was her daughter's body stabbed 17 times in her own bed. Forensics indicated that she had been raped twice prior to being stabbed.

Their pictures on the five o'clock news verified that the name of the deceased was indeed the girl I was remembering. She and her mom hadn't been in church for a while so I had to double check my records to see which block she lived on before going to their house.

Quite a crowd had gathered out along the curb. Flowers and stuffed animals had already begun to be piled high on the sidewalk in front of the downstairs window. I worked my way through those milling and those loitering in search of a familiar face.

The mom was visiting with everyone until she saw me. At that point, she grabbed hold of me and wept. My legs held both of us upright.

Several minutes later a Cadillac pulled up to the curb. Our city council representative emerged to express her condolences. At that point, the mom released her grip and again began visiting with the growing crowd.

The day's heat and humidity hung heavy in the air. The crowd was restless and its agitation was growing. It felt like things were on the verge of going out of control. I didn't know what to do so I went home and kept my other appointments previously scheduled for that evening.

I think this is the point in the da 'votion where I'm supposed to connect the story to some more universal principal. I'm supposed to point out the Spirit's action or the role of the Church or something like that.

I'm not that smart. Making sense of what happened is well beyond my understanding of God and the capacity of the English language.

I do, however, need to go back in my mind to that night once in a while. I don't go back to it to try to figure it out any more. The world doesn't fit neatly into the boxes we construct. Like the writer of Ecclesiastes, I sometimes need to just acknowledge the senselessness of the human condition and choose faith in the midst of it.

God, I don't understand things most of the time. In the midst of senselessness, help me to choose You.

DONKEY

We were reading the story of Palm Sunday together with some teenage boys. The kids had just read how Jesus had sent some disciples into the village to get a donkey for him to ride. When we read that they had put some clothes on the back of the donkey before Jesus got on, the group leader asked, "Why do you think they did that?"

Without hesitation and in all seriousness, one of the boys honestly answered, "So no one would know that it was the one they had just stolen." The others all agreed.

That was NOT the answer I was expecting.

I would have probably answered that the disciples put some of their clothes on the donkey to make something like a saddle for Jesus or to somehow honor Him. The thought of the disciples trying to disguise that donkey had never crossed my mind.

But the disguise made sense in the context of the kids' world and my ideas made sense in the context of my world. The fact of the matter is, though, that we were both probably wrong.

I will never fully understand the context of the stories of ancient Palestine. I can read about it. I can study it. I can travel to modern Israel and Palestine. I can try really really really hard and I can get better at interpreting scripture because of my efforts. I can become quite knowledgeable of the context and through that I can gain deeper insights into the text.

Still, I will never fully experience much less understand the context of the stories of Jesus because I'm a relatively affluent white man in the USA 2000 years after all these events took place. I would guess that my understandings would sound even more off base to the original hearers than the kids' idea of eluding authorities by disguising a donkey sounded to me.

Yet, somewhere in the midst of my lack there is Truth. Truth seeks to reveal Himself through the text. And as His people gather for serious study, when they bring with them enough humility to know that they will never really understand even a syllable without the Spirit's help, Truth is revealed despite our context. It comes humbly as it rides in on a donkey.

And I'm not so sure why that donkey has some clothes laid on its back.

Lord, humble me with your Word. Help me welcome the Truth from it that You give into my life.

RETURNED

Every once in a while when I get to the church there will be a couple of old Bibles leaning up next to the door. No note. No name. Just a Bible or two that a neighbor has left in front of the church.

Invariably, these Bibles are in rough condition. They've been folded in odd ways or pages are missing or they're especially musty. They may have even become rain-soaked since arriving at the church door.

No matter their condition, I always take them in.

What I've discovered is that people don't know what to do with an old Bible, especially if it has somehow gotten damaged. Maybe it got musty in a box buried deep in the dark, damp basement full of junk. Maybe the cheap paperback binding didn't hold up. Maybe it got bent and creased when it was used to hold up that old, comfortable sofa.

No matter how it happened, once a Bible gets damaged, people aren't sure what to do. It just doesn't seem right to throw it in the recycle bin. The content hasn't changed and it somehow seems wrong to just put it out with the newspapers and junk mail.

So they bring the Bible to the church, leaving it at the foot of the door. Somehow in their minds, returning the book's content to its source provides absolution for their neglect of it and hope that it might do someone else some good in the future.

An old Bible is hard for me to deal with, too.

In it are stories I learned as a child and that I teach the kids in the neighborhood today. Yet, when I go back and read them again the lessons are not so clear and the picture the stories paint of God isn't always the same as the one I've painted of Him in my mind.

In it is a repeated call to abandon the ways of the world and to live fully human in light of the Gospel. Yet, I want to live in the light of the Gospel while only abandoning a few of the world's ways, namely the ones that I already don't like anyway.

In it are stories and words and guidance that I just don't understand. I want to either shape them to my own liking or to discard them. Yet, it's the parts of *me* that refuse to let go and be shaped by the text into *His* liking that need to be discarded.

What should I do with the old contents of the Bible, written all over my heart and mind? Some of it I've let get musty by boxing it up in the dark damp places inside me where I store my junk. Sometimes, like cheap binding, I haven't held very tight to it. Most often, though, I've misused it to prop up something comfortable for my spirit to rest on like an old sofa.

Yes, it's hard for me to deal with my old Bible. And many (most?) days I just want to leave it out of sight and get on with my daily tasks. But when the words inside me get folded in odd ways or are missing some pages or get musty I've learned from my neighbors what to do.

I need to take it back to the Source. I put it on the ground before Him. There I can receive absolution for the past and hope for His word's work in me in the future.

No matter the condition of His word in me, He'll always take me in.

Lord, shape me with your Word. Let your mystery not confound me but draw me closer to You.

TRUNK

The funeral did not go well.

From beginning to end, one thing after another went wrong in ways I could not have imagined. It wasn't the funeral home's fault. It wasn't the family's fault. It wasn't my fault. It just did NOT go well.

It wasn't only my opinion, either. While at the cemetery, the funeral director turned to me and in his most compassionate, professional, somber, funeral home voice said me, "I'm thinking of climbing into the trunk of the limo until this is over. Would you care to join me?"

Yes, it was that bad.

And in that moment, being secluded from everyone and everything carried great appeal, even if it meant being in the limo's dark trunk.

The desire to hide in a dark place is quite familiar to me. It's not unusual to have seasons when multiple things go horribly wrong. It's no one's fault; they just happen. And there's no sense in trying to find the good in its midst at that moment. It is what it is, and my usual desire is to find a dark place to hide from the cascading trauma.

Back at the cemetery, the offer for some time in the

trunk of a limo seemed like a great option. The funeral director and I both decided, though, to stay out in the sunlight with the bereaved. The best help we could give was to be present amid the chaos.

It's in those times of wanting to crawl into a trunk that I need to remember that Jesus is Immanuel ---- *God with Us*. He chooses to be fully present in all our circumstances. If I follow Him I'll end up being present in all kinds of situations, too.

So I have a choice. I can be present in people's lives or I can hide, be it in the trunk of a car or in a dark place deep inside myself somewhere.

Though the dark places sometimes seem most appealing, being present in and with the Light is where I am called to be.

Lord, help me overcome fears and inadequacies that I may stand firmly in Your presence and be fully present in the lives of others.

BIRTH

Our first child was born while we were living in the suburbs. Our second child was born while we were living in the inner-city. The different settings made for totally different experiences.

For example, when living in the 'burbs, the Andersons were having a baby. While living in da 'hood, my wife was having a baby. That may sound subtle, but it played out in quite a variety of ways.

This was made clear even before the baby was born. On more than one occasion when telling someone of the pregnancy, I was asked, "Who's the father?"

Wow! ---- in sooooo many ways.

That question is normally the first question asked about a pregnancy in the 'hood. For that matter, it's usually a piece of information that people might not know. But you would think that people who know me and/or my wife could have skipped that question and gone on to more productive conversation. For a moment, I guess they forgot who they were talking to.

Sometimes I think about my own prayer time and the questions I ask God. They make sense to me and are the kind that are normally asked in my world. But if I would stop for half a second before I start talking and remember who I'm talking to, I could skip to more productive conversation rather than ask some questions that would cause "Wow! ----- in sooooo many ways" to reverberate across the heavenly realm.

I ask "Where are you, God?" when I know He has already promised to be with me always. I ask "What should I do?" without first considering how his Word is a lamp unto my feet and a light unto my path. I ask "God, why don't you _____?" even though I know that my thoughts are not His thoughts and my ways are not His ways.

Fortunately, I also know that I live in His grace. Being born into this world is a totally different experience from being born into life in Christ. The first happened many years ago in a sterile hospital environment with doctors and nurses and a crib and crocheted baby booties waiting for me. The second continues to take place each moment in a messy world that's not always hospitable or accommodating to this new creation.

And when it's all over, my hope is that no one will have to ask about me, "Who's his Father?"

Thank you, Lord, for your grace. Help me to always remember who You are.

TERMINAL

He lamented the same topic each time we visited. His girlfriend had a terminal illness.

I never met his girlfriend; I never knew her name. I don't know where she lived, though he was basically homeless so I'm not sure how that all worked anyway. Occasionally he would ask that I remember her in prayer.

The thing with her illness was that, though there was no cure, her death from it was not expected any time soon. In fact, the disease didn't have a direct obvious impact on her physical well being. She was in the very early stages of this slowly progressing illness and the doctors had predicted it would have minimal impact on her for the next 10 years. The prognosis was for gradual decline after that. Since she was already in her late 50s, with mindful monitoring she would most likely live for what most people would consider a full life.

None of this seemed to matter to him, though. The fact that she had a terminal illness obsessed his mind and depleted his well-being.

One day as he again lamented about the situation, I turned to him and was surprised to hear the following statement come out of my mouth:

"You know, we're all terminal. She just knows what from."

He gave me an odd look and changed the topic of conversation.

I saw him again about a week later. He looked about 2 inches taller and 10 years younger. His demeanor, actions, and conversation were filled with a new vitality. In our visits from that time forward he no longer obsessed about the terminal nature of his girlfriend's illness. He would occasionally mention that her illness was terminal but always followed it with a grin and the words, " . . . but, we all are."

That little statement changed his life for the better. When I remember it, my life is better, too.

There are only a few material things like pyramids and Great Walls and Coliseums that have survived the ages and they're mostly in some state of ruin. Virtually all of the music ever composed or words ever written will never be heard again. The churches that Paul helped establish are not mega-churches or beacons of Christianity today.

Some might find that depressing. For me it's a relief. It takes the pressure off of me and reorders priorities. Sermons and public prayers change from speaking words today for all eternity to speaking eternal words for today. Building a church that will endure changes from setting things up now that will be right forever to forever setting things up that will be right for now.

Ministry comes not in monuments but in moments, and moments are fleeting. We're all terminal -- our works, our ideas, our selves.

And just once in a while I have a day when I'm not obsessively lamenting that fact. It's then that I can let the One who was and is and is to come fully invade and embrace His terminal creation known as me, bringing with Him into this fleeting moment the vitality of His everlasting life.

Thank you, God, for each moment. Free me from my focus on the temporary to live fully in Your presence.

TEMPTATION

I don't remember exactly which chapter and verse we were reading with the teens at church that night. But the word "temptation" was in it. So I asked, "What's a temptation."

Only one kid raised his hand so I called on him. He stood up, shuffled his feet, swayed, snapped his fingers, and said, "It's a guy who dances like this while he's singing."

The others all agreed.

I'm not sure which surprised me more:

1. That he gave that answer.
2. That he and the others honestly agreed that it was the right answer.
3. That all the kids were so familiar with the singing group The Temptations.

Needless to say, we explored another meaning of the word temptation that night. Once we did, the passage seemed to make a little more sense to the kids.

That was good because understanding different kinds of temptations can help make sense of the root of our own motivations.

As a church we've pontificated on the classic sex,

drugs, and rock 'n roll types of temptations to the point that sometimes the church is viewed by the world as simply the group who is against those things. And yes, they can be quite tempting.

We also talk about the temptations that impact our behavior when we're angry or mad or hungry. They're not as scandalous as the other temptations but are very real and are sometimes addressed.

But for me the real temptations that get me in trouble are the ones more subtle. See, it's tempting for me to only do the kinds of ministry that I know people will express gratitude for instead of all the things that need to be done that no one seems to appreciate. It's tempting for me to use the business of doing good works as an excuse to not take the time to delve deeper into my relationship with God. It's tempting for me to quickly make doable plans and try to get heaven's endorsement rather than go the through the discernment process and take faith risks to reveal and implement God's plans. It's tempting for me to say, "God answered my prayer" when He did what I wanted rather than looking for how He answered amid my not getting my way.

Though these types of temptations don't grab as high of ratings as the ones featured on daytime television talk shows, they are just as destructive because they have the same root. That root is a self-centeredness that warps the words of Jesus when it cries out, "My kingdom come, my will be done on earth as it is in my heaven."

When I get to facing those temptations that are complicated, personal, and not likely to end up getting me arrested or fired, I usually prefer to shuffle my feet, sway, and snap my fingers in hopes that they will all just go away. And the culture around me seems to agree that this is the right answer.

But I have a God who loves me. I've asked Him to take over my life, and not just the parts that grab the headlines but the fine print, too. Knowing that, then, my prayer this day can be,

Suffer us not to be lead into temptation, but deliver us from evil. For Thine is the kingdom and the power and the glory forever and ever. Amen. (Matthew 6:13)

GLOW

She wanted her baby to receive its sacramental blessing right away. Though they had only been home from the hospital a day or two she was eager to have it done.

The next event on the calendar was our Christmas Eve service so we decided to have the blessing then. That evening we filled the small storefront church with candles, creating a peaceful light while at the same time dimming the scary and dangerous effects of the dilapidated room in which we gathered.

There amid the warm glow of both the candles and the season she brought her baby for its blessing. Those who gathered shared in the Spirit during that time together and congratulated the mother on the good choice she made to have the baby blessed that night.

It was a moving Christmas Eve for us all, especially since we were well aware that in a matter of days Child Protective Services would be permanently removing the baby from her mother.

Mom had already endangered the child for nine months prior to the birth by using heroin throughout the pregnancy. The current home that she had for the baby was not a safe or healthy place even when mom was lucent.

But that night she made the right choice. She thoroughly loved her baby and did not willingly give her to the state. The choice to bring this child before God and submit to His love took great courage. Our compassion both for mother and child underscored the need to put the whole situation into hands bigger and more capable than our own.

The Prince of Peace was with mother and child that night. He was with all of us who were both entangled and torn in the midst of this very difficult situation.

And we live in faith that His blessing continues to be upon that child, providing both a peaceful Light while at the same time dimming the scary and dangerous effects of the room in which the child spent the days before her birth.

Be near me Lord Jesus I ask Thee to stay
Close by me forever and love me I pray.
Bless all the dear children in Thy tender care.
And fit us for heaven to live with Thee there.
       --- Anonymous

NEWS

It was a dark and stormy night. Actually, it was only dark outside. I've just always wanted to start a story that way.

Through much of the day we'd been installing a new laminate floor in the church. We had worked together and had ample opportunities to practice the fruit of the Spirit with one another, especially patients, kindness, and self-control.

And long suffering.

The directions were more complicated than we originally thought. Some of my personal power tools had been stolen when we turned our backs for just a few seconds. The materials were backbreakingly heavy. Dirt and scraps were everywhere. Sawdust stuck to our skin.

The project was about 80% complete that Saturday evening with three services scheduled for Sunday. We would not be able to finish in time. We came to a reasonable stopping point and called it quits. That night I went back to the church alone to try to set up a few things for morning and to finish the sermon, now only 14 hours away.

It was then that he just opened the door and walked in like he owned the place. I knew who he was as he had lived up the street from the church for many years. But I don't recall having said anything more personal to him than things like, "beautiful evening tonight" when we'd passed on the street. I think a couple of his grandkids might have been to a festival the church hosted once. I wasn't sure of his name.

He said, "I saw the lights on so I came in because I knew you'd want to hear my good news." This was followed by an overly detailed and graphic description of the hunting trip he'd been on that day. He got a deer.

After congratulating him I said, "And you have perfect timing, too. You got here just as I was going to try to get this refrigerator back in place. Can you help me for a minute?" He gladly did. We got the refrigerator out of the middle of the room then he headed back into the night to go home and share both his news and, in the near future, some cuts of meat with his neighbors.

Though sore and tired, bespeckled with sawdust, and still a little disgusted about the stolen tools, hope was refreshed in me. Because for just a few minutes, the temporal reflected my hope in the things less easy to quantify.

My hope is that the church is a place where Light shines out into the surrounding darkness beckoning people to come in.

My hope is that the church is known as a place where people can come with Good News to share.

My hope is that the church will follow the Good News with opportunities to serve.

My hope is that the church will release people back into the world to continue sharing the Good News and to bless others from their bounty.

And sometimes just a glimpse of hope in the temporal gives me just enough Breath to buy new tools, set up the chairs, and blow away the personal thunderclouds on what could have been a very dark and stormy night.

Lord, thank you for the hope you've placed in us. Help me to hang onto it amid each day's challenges.

ANSWER

She had been coming to church for only a few months and everything was new and exciting. She was five years old and had never heard any of the Bible stories we were sharing each Sunday afternoon.

She came all four weeks of Advent and was shocked, amazed, and delighted to learn that Christmas had something to do with Jesus. For four weeks in a row our themes, lessons, and crafts all shouted the message, "Christmas is Jesus' Birthday!"

So on the first Sunday after Christmas her hand was the fastest one in the air when I asked about why we celebrate Christmas. With a giant smile and total delight from knowing the right answer, she called out,

"PRESENTS!"

Everyone on staff sank just a little bit as I redirected the conversation to get the name "Jesus" to somehow be affiliated with the celebration of Christmas. Maybe next year she'll get it right.

Though I was truly disappointed that she didn't get the right answer, her honesty was refreshing. So often I'm smart enough to give the right answers to questions at church. They aren't, though, always quite as honest.

Some of the right answers I know include:

-Christmas is all about Jesus' birth.
-I need to be patient and wait upon the Lord.
-With God all things are possible.
-All things work together for good for those who love the Lord and are called according to His purposes.

I give these and other "right" answers for several reasons. First, the bright side of me knows they are correct and I answer in hopes of building my faith a bit. The darker side of me, though, knows that most other people at church already know the "right" answer and I don't want to look even more foolish or shallow than I normally do. In addition, I don't need yet another person to talk down to me to teach me the "right" answer that I already know anyway.

Maybe it would be good if I sometimes said out loud that some years Christmas is more about a couple days out of town with the family than a manger scene, that I get tired of waiting on the Lord and occasionally plan a hostile takeover, and that I believe the problems in front of me are both completely impossible and cannot in any way be used for good.

If I were more like an eager five-year-old child I would raise my hand and confess these wrong-but-honest answers, inside myself and maybe even in front of the other kids in my class. Who knows? It might open up an opportunity for God to redirect the conversation to help the right answer be the honest answer.

Maybe next year I'll *really* get it right.

God, help me be more honest with myself and with You. Use this to help me live more fully in your Truth.

KEYS

The keys were just hanging there. Apparently, someone had unlocked the door and left the keys in the lock when they went inside. All their treasures -- the house, the car, and who-knows-what else -- were now available to strangers just for the taking.

I happened upon this scene when I was delivering fliers one morning. I'm sure the keys hadn't been in the lock very long because some people, casually loitering across the street, seemed to be looking for a clearing in the foot traffic so they could find an opportunity to help themselves to the treasures those keys provided.

So I knocked on the door. No one replied. I knocked again. Still nothing. I knocked harder. Cussing came out but the owner didn't. I knocked again.

The door flew open and I was in the shadow of a very large, angry, burly man. He was not happy and proceeded to loudly tell me so. The collar I was wearing, I believe, saved me from some even more colorful language than what I was already getting.

Without a chance to get a word in I just pointed at the keys. He glanced at his door. Then he LOOKED at his door and quit talking.

He took the keys out of the lock and looked across

the street at the loiterers who were now casually dispersing.

He started talking again, only these were words of thanks and relief from fear and panic from what might have happened had I not been persistent or had he not come to the door.

I wish I could say that I didn't know how this guy felt. I do stupid things all the time. I'm oblivious to many of the mistakes I make and would be horrified if I recognized the consequences.

And so I need to be open to having someone knock on my door and offer correction. Honest, thoughtful correction isn't the enemy; it's just a friend I might want to yell at.

Now, just because someone knocks on my door doesn't mean they have my best interest in mind. People knock on my door all the time looking to sell me meat out of the back of their truck. Or it might be someone at the wrong house looking for my neighbor. Or it might be someone asking for money. Maybe you don't have this problem, but I have an abundance of people who have wonderful plans for my life if only I would do things their way.

But when honest correction with my interest at heart comes knocking, I best look at where it's pointing. It will show me the keys that I didn't know I was missing that unlock the treasures God has in store for me.

Thank you, Lord, for loving me enough to not leave me as I am. Correct me and help me to accept and implement Your wisdom and truth in my life.

GENERATIONS

After being cussed out by a dad who didn't appreciate the fact that his daughter had been in a church, much less that she participated often enough to earn a trip to the church's summer camp, I headed to the next house to try to get parental permission for a different kid to spend a week at camp. On the short walk from one house to the next, I stopped on the corner to visit with some kids who had been to camp in the past. They were all dealing drugs so my visit slowed their commerce for a few minutes.

The futility of the situation didn't improve when mom answered the door at the next kid's house. She was clearly strung out on heroin and nodded off as I talked with her.

Until she heard the word "camp," that is. Once that little word came out of my mouth she connected. Not with me, but I could see she was off in a different space than where heroin usually takes someone.

She turned to me and interrupted saying, "When I was a kid I went to a camp with a church one summer. I want my boy to do that, too." She signed the forms.

It's so easy for me to get caught up in today. So much of life seems to be an exercise in banging my head against a wall followed by people complaining that I didn't bang it hard enough to do any good. And when I look just at today (and maybe the last couple of years) then I can only agree.

But that mom's lucid moment forced me to refocus through the eternal lens that disciples of Jesus are privileged to have. The woman's life was clearly a mess, but the faithfulness of the church of her childhood was opening doors for her son's future that might not have been otherwise open to him.

And when I can look through that lens I have just a bit of hope. That hope is not for today but for her grandchildren and great-grandchildren. I think of what could happen if Jesus' disciples will continue to surround and bless this family for generations to come. Is it possible that each generation could grow just a bit closer to Christ than the last? Could a family's testimony of growing in Christ from generation to generation empower disciples for generations to come?

When I look through that eternal lens, I can have some hope that the former campers who were dealing drugs that afternoon will not only let their kids come to church and go to camp but will encourage them to do so.

And I can hope that the girl whose dad cussed me out because she was in church got enough good seed planted in her so that she won't cuss out the pastor who comes by ten summers from now inviting her four and six year old kids to a week of Vacation Bible School.

Because my God has plans for this world that are bigger than the span of my life. I get the privilege and responsibility of remaining faithful and being a blessing in this generation, trusting that other people of faith will build on those blessings in the generations to come.

Lord, let me look through Your eyes that I may see the worth You've put in each person and the hope You have for them and their descendants.

MEMORABLE

A friend joined me in the little space by the bathrooms for prayer. I was getting ready to both preside and preach at the evening's worship session after having already presided and preached a different sermon at the morning service then taught the lesson and led the crafts at Kids' Church that afternoon. I was tired and needed all the prayer I could get.

And it was one of those prayer sessions when I KNEW that God was moving in response to my friend's prayer. "Oh Lord, we ask that this be a memorable service . . ." That was all I heard.

All I wanted was a smooth plain vanilla lots of smiles short prayers no real problems service where nothing too earth-shattering happened so I could go home, eat dinner, and get to bed.

But he prayed for a memorable service. I resisted the urge to scream, "TAKE IT BACK TAKE IT BACK TAKE IT BACK!" That would have been rude and useless because I knew God and would be answering soon.

And, yes, of all the services I've been a part of, this one was definitely rises to the top of the list of memorable.

During the opening song and only seconds after the

"Amen" to my friend's prayer, I had to physically remove three teenage boys who began verbally harassing and physically threatening a senior citizen who was sitting in the back row.

Because of trouble on the steps in front of the church we had to lock the doors and post a bouncer to control who could come in during the rest of the service.

After a song about peace, one woman who had recently started attending services stood up, turned around, and loudly cussed out some kids who were sitting several rows behind her.

And as the service drew to a close, a woman raised her hand and said, "Tonight I've decided to get baptized. How soon can we do it?"

We set the date.

Yes, it was a memorable service. And it wasn't so much because of the utter bedlam inside and out. The fact that He moved in a life-transforming way in someone even in the midst of that chaos -- now *THAT* is memorable.

I spend a lot of time praying for all the insanity in my life to just stop. And when I've maxed out on all the craziness I think I can handle, all I can seem to pray is for God to please just let me go home, eat dinner, and go to bed.

It's then that I also need to look around and see if a raised hand is trying to get my attention to let me know that God is doing something memorable in the very middle of it.

Because people have been praying in churches and in temples and at home and on the streets and even by the bathroom doors asking God to do something memorable. And though the chaos seems bent on distracting us, God is bringing transformation to people right in the center of the madness.

And on those days that I can realize that I *KNOW* I walk in the midst of prayers that are being answered, it's the glimpses of those answers rather than the chaos that make the day memorable.

Father, help me see you working in the world around me. Let me witness of You and share in Your vision.

QUIT

"Get out of this church and NEVER come back!" I yelled at the kids as I shoved them out the door. I closed the blinds, set the alarm, locked the door, and marched home. As I came through the door of my house carrying several boxes of untouched pizza with me, my wife remarked that I was home earlier than usual. I replied, "I quit --- and I'm GLAD!"

Not my finest ministry moment.

The kids had come into the second session of Pizza Church loudly bossing me around and complaining about how much pizza they thought they deserved. Between the first and second sessions the kids gathered outside were fighting, yelling, and causing a scene that made all the neighbors nervous and regretful that the church was on their block. The first session was full of kids who were snarky with me and each other.

And just before all this started the other person who was to be on staff that night canceled so I was the only grown-up in the room.

The kids were sure surprised the next week when they showed up and I didn't. I had already been scheduled to be out of town and those who were filling in had been advised of the previous week's events. They leveraged my absence for all it was worth.

It was then that the kids began to take the situation seriously. They started to figure out that I would be back when I was ready to come back, not when they demanded. They started to figure out that there are lines that cannot be intentionally and repeatedly crossed without consequences. They started to figure out that if we were to continue together it would be based on an appropriate and healthy relationship with me and with each other.

And when I got back in town I returned to the youth group again. Things didn't change instantly; I said that the kids *started* to figure things out. But there was just enough movement in the right direction to give us some space to regroup and move forward.

So I have to wonder how often Jesus is talking specifically to me when I read from Matthew 17:17 (CEV) in which He said, "How much longer must I be with you? Why do I have to put up with you?"

I sometimes get a bossy attitude with Him about the things I think I deserve. If I'm not careful my behavior and interactions can draw negative attention from those around me and have them questioning if they want Him around. My cynicism leads to snarkiness with Him and with those who are trying to serve Him.

So once in a while I need a time out. It's then that I start to take things seriously again. I start to figure out that I don't have "God on Demand" but that I'm on His agenda. I start to figure out that there are negative consequences to my behaviors and attitudes if I repeatedly and intentionally go to those dark places. And I start to figure out that life in God's Kingdom is about living in an appropriate and healthy relationship with Him and with those around me.

I'm glad He doesn't kick me out telling me to never come back the way I did with the kids. And I'm glad that he's patient with me so I can be in "start to" mode over and over again.

By the way, in being true to character, all of those kids who I told to leave and never come back utterly refused to do what I said. Every last one of them kept coming to church. They would not give up.

I think that might be an indicator as to who the grown-ups in the room were.

Thank you, Jesus, for your abundant grace. Help me grow in relationship with you and with those around me.

CRAZY

It's not that she was *completely* crazy. Actually, she was quite functional in her life. But it was clear to everyone (except for her, of course) that she needed her meds just a little more than the rest of us need ours.

So I wasn't surprised one afternoon as I was walking by her house when she flagged me down to share something that didn't seem completely right to me.

"Pastor! The street lights! They're really, really bright now! I mean, I sit out on my steps every night but last night I could hardly stand it when the traffic light changed from green to yellow and red and back to green. And the crosswalk signs, too. I mean, they're all just so bright!"

She was a bit panicked and needed some assurance that the world wasn't coming to an end. After our chat she seemed to feel better but wasn't completely satisfied. I moved along in my day and soon forgot about the conversation.

But when I was out walking in the dark I remembered it. I noticed that the lights *were* brighter. A LOT brighter! And not just the ones by her house but on every street corner in the neighborhood. And no one else out that night seemed to notice, much less be bothered by it.

The 11:00 newscast rescued both of us from our distress. We learned that the city had started at our end of town in converting all the stoplights from incandescent to LED in hopes of saving energy. Our peace was restored.

Just like what happened with that morning's conversation, it's easy for me to not really remember what people say when they think a little differently than I do. I can consciously or subconsciously dismiss what someone says based on gender, education, race, culture, IQ, theology, socioeconomic standing, and a myriad of other "qualifiers" that are wired into my brain.

When I can recognize this, I need to have a bright yellow or flashing red light come on at the intersection of my synapses. I'm not saying that all expressed thoughts and ideas are equally valid; I just need to make sure I don't dismiss them because the speaker seems a little crazy to me. There may be some truth in there that I have yet to see.

Because that's what the folks did to people like Isaiah and Jeremiah. Both of these men came across to others as basically functional but in need of some meds. Yet, *they* were the ones who saw the bright new Light before the rest did. But instead of listening, the people had to take a walk in the darkness before they remembered what these men had tried to tell them.

I wonder what God is trying to reveal to me today and if I am unwilling to hear it just because of the vessel He is using to convey it. I hope I can see His brightness before I need an 11th hour rescue to have my peace restored.

Lord, help me to be open to your Truth. Remove my blinders that I might see You.

FAILURE

I wanted him to die.

That was a new feeling for me. It wasn't because he had done anything particularly bad to me. It wasn't that I even disliked him. As he lay in his bed gasping for air I wanted him to stop fighting and just let it all end.

I could hardly stand to be in the room much less look at him. In that bed I saw our world's failures.

The failure of the medical system was in that bed. The multiple diseases that ravaged his body had been left to progress or had received minimal care as he had no insurance and no way to pay.

The failure of social services was in that bed. He easily qualified for a variety of community services but was unable to negotiate the system. By the time I met him, he had given up trying for some services and had become paranoid of the rest.

The failure of the free market was in that bed. He'd never been quite good enough for the jobs that were out there. His limited intellectual capacity and an occasional fight at work were more than supervisors were willing to put up with. He was too smart to get into service programs but not smart enough to make it through job training.

The failure of mental health care was in that bed. If I had lived the repeatedly traumatic life he did, I would need counseling and meds. He received neither. His DNA didn't help the situation, either. Plus he was smart enough to know that the system could inflict more anguish than what he was experiencing outside of it.

The failure of our school system was in that bed. He had been shuffled through and passed along and given a custodial education until he was old enough to drop out. He never had any reason to look back after his 16th birthday.

The failure of his family was in that bed. They were especially gifted in reinforcing bad behaviors and inflicting guilt to manipulate others. They were all able to survive but none were able to thrive.

The failure of the church was in that bed. He had come to us many times for help. We had tried to welcome him into the fellowship. We were never able to help enough to make much of a difference other than an occasional meal. His temper challenged the group's need for safety.

As he looked up at me, gasping for one of his last breaths, I -- we -- society, were all failing him once again. And in the darkness of my mind I somehow convinced myself that once he died the problems would die with him and we could all continue on with our little comfortable lives. If all these failures were to go away, then he needed to go away.

But the volunteer hospice nurse kept coming through the room. She didn't know all the problems that lead up to this point or, if she did, she didn't seem to be too worried about them. She simply provided dignity and honor and care. She even stayed on after her shift ended for the day just to help out. For once in his life someone was making sure that he would not be failed again.

And she didn't seem too worried about the time of death. That would be handled by the One who had the next shift. For on her shift, like mine, she needed to be present and create a place of dignity for a stranger in need.

When I was hungry, you gave me something to eat, and when I was thirsty, you gave me something to drink. When I was a stranger, you welcomed me, and when I was naked, you gave me clothes to wear. When I was sick, you took care of me, and when I was in jail, you visited me. Whenever you did it for any of my people, no matter how unimportant they seemed, you did it for me. (Matthew 25:35-36, 40 CEV)

For a few hours at the end of his life he began to experience the healing and restoring welcome of the Christ that he would soon receive in its fullness.

And he didn't take the failings with him. Instead he left them here so that I -- we -- society might be blessed with repentance and grace and dependence on an undying Love that never fails.

Lord, let me recognize Your grace and mercy upon me as I go through this day. Help me live it out by fully welcoming others as I would You.

SWIMMING

"Swimming!"

That's the nearly unanimous answer I get when I ask kids the question, "What was your favorite part of youth camp?" After 51 weeks full of prayer, fundraising, community organizing, coordinating with camp directors, hunting down parents for signatures on forms, renting vans or a bus, driving back and forth through Washington DC traffic, and the myriad of other things we do all year to get kids out of the neighborhood and into a potentially life-changing week out of the city with unique activities and powerful encounters with God, their favorite part of the week was the swimming.

So, while jammed in crawling traffic on I-95 for hour number three of the 78 mile drive home, I start to think that next year my life would be happier and the kids' lives would be just as good if, instead of camp, I rented the pool at the YMCA for a couple of hours and let them all just swim.

But then there was that one kid one year who didn't say "swimming." He said, "'votions."

At first I didn't know what he was talking about. He clarified, "You know, them votions we do in the cabin each night. Them was my favorite thing at camp."

"What made them your favorite?"

"Well, we's all still and quiet and stuff and we get to talk a little and think a lot about God and life and, you know, stuff like that. It's like God is so real there and we know we're all gonna be OK."

The other boys in the van piped in, "Yeah, I liked that, too. We don't get to do stuff like that when we're at home."

When I've been blessed with the opportunity to get far away from my world for a few days, I must confess that my first response when asked about the trip usually has something to do with a bargain price or free upgrade (or both!) on a rental car, hotel room or airline ticket. No matter how many amazing places He lets me go or activities He lets me experience, my first words of praise are usually about a travel bargain.

Does He sometimes think, "Next year I'll just help him find a deal on a convertible at BWI and he can drive around the Beltway a couple of times"?

I'm pretty sure He doesn't think that way. But early in my conversations it wouldn't hurt to acknowledge the blessing of time to think about God and life and, you know, stuff like that which help me know that God is so real and that I'm gonna be OK.

Of course, if I do, then I'll be in some deeper

conversation than I might want to have at that moment. Plus, after some true encounters with the Holy I need time to process my experiences before I can put words to them. And besides, the whole thing wouldn't have been near as fun without the great deal on the rental car.

Just like camp wouldn't be near as fun without time at the pool. Plus it takes time for kids to put words to their camp experiences. And in the van on their way home they're tired and dirty and hungry and sad to be leaving which isn't exactly a time when any of us want to delve into deeper conversation.

Swimming.

It's a good answer. Plus I know that once laundry is done and there's been a couple of good night's rest and we're sitting around the table with a bowls of ice cream or slices of pizza, the conversations might just give some hints that the 51 weeks full of prayer, fundraising, community organizing, coordinating with camp directors, hunting down parents for signatures on forms, renting vans or a bus, driving back and forth through Washington DC traffic, and the myriad of other things we did actually provided some life-changing opportunities to swim out into the deep with God.

Lord, let the praise of You that is in my heart be on my lips and in my deeds that all might see and know Your goodness.

SCAREY

Six shots rang out as I was shutting down the computer for the night. I pulled on my shoes and followed the flow of people to the corner of S. Carey and James Streets, arriving before the police. There his lifeless, bloodied body lay crumpled in the street.

S. Carey and James.

It's the same corner where the police shot an unarmed man a couple years back. That happened right after the girl got hit and killed by a car at that same corner.

It's where several prostitutes gather with their toddlers in the evening, rotating who is with the johns and who is on the street watching the kids as they wait for Mom's return.

Sometimes on those same steps during daylight hours I see junkies nodding off after their heroin fix.

From S. Carey and James I can see two different houses in which people died and no one knew it for over a week until the smell alerted the neighbors.

It's also where I have witnessed a couple of street brawls.

The house three in from the corner has been fixed up

since it was fire bombed shortly after I moved to this neighborhood.

The building across the street from that house is where the boys used to wait for the pedophiles to come by and offer them money for favors.

Of course, at the next intersection north I can show you the house where the father threw his infant down the stairs in order to kill her (which he did successfully) and at the next intersection south I can point out open air drug deals and blatant prostitution both day and night.

Meanwhile, we'll be gathering in churches around the globe to debate the color of carpeting in the foyer, who is qualified to receive communion, and what songs are appropriate to sing in a particular service. Denominations are spending countless dollars and hours gathering people to decide things like who can be ordained to serve in ministry and will spend even more money and time when churches split over these and other issues. People will be in an uproar about the location of a mosque and riot over football games.

Yet corners like S. Carey and James keep happening in places all over the globe. Unnoticed. Undebated. Unfunded.

The people around the world trapped in places like S. Carey and James wonder who will lead the riot, the uproar, the debate on their behalf. Who will bring healing and wholeness and restoration to their land? Who will bring hope and peace and sweat and tears and presence to not let another shot ring out, not let another john pick up, or bomb crash through the glass?

Yes, it's easier to talk about new carpeting because there's hope we might just be able to solve the problem. But if the church doesn't look at S. Carey and James with hope, who will? Who even could?

Do we have a Creator who is unsatisfied with the conditions at S. Carey and James? Do we have a Savior who wants both spiritual and temporal salvation at S. Carey and James? Do we have a Sustainer who will give strength and wisdom and courage to those who will follow His lead to S. Carey and James?

S. Carey and James. The locals say SCarey Street, and scary it can be.

Good thing God's Spirit doesn't make cowards of us (2 Timothy 1:7).

Lord, let my life shine Your light in the darkness.

HAPPY

I was a little nervous about meeting her husband. She and I had been exchanging emails and making plans for several weeks. I wasn't sure what her husband thought of his wife's and my new relationship and he had me asked to meet him in the parking lot of a shopping center just off the interstate.

He greeted me with by saying, "Thank you so much for what you've done for my wife." He went on to say that the things that make her especially happy include finding bargains and shopping for school supplies. Based on that information, she must have been a VERY happy person for much of the summer.

By scouring the sales fliers and engaging in strategic shopping for several weeks, she'd been buying up all the best deals on school supplies and sharing that information with me. Her husband's pickup bed was now full of crayons and notebooks and erasers and glue sticks and all kinds of things kids need to start the school year right. Through this she'd become by far that year's biggest contributor to our school supply drive at the church.

And the happiness just kept flowing. She was happy to shop. Her husband was happy to deliver her treasures. I was happy to distribute them to kids in the neighborhood. The kids and their parents were happy to receive them. The teachers were happy to have kids show up with what they needed to learn.

Who knows where (or if) that chain of happiness ends? I do know that some of the kids who received supplies that year are now the first in their families to attend college.

I often get overwhelmed and grumpy with the magnitude of the tasks at helping bring transformation to the place where I occupy. It's good for me to remember, though, that sometimes all it takes is someone to simply get happily excited about finding a box of crayons for a dime. It starts a chain reaction bringing enough joy and hope for one more day, or week, or marking period, or semester, or school year which, in time, transforms the world for generations to come.

Lord, let Your JOY be my strength.

TURKEY

It's been our congregation's tradition to have a "dessert only" potluck the Sunday evening before Thanksgiving. Everyone brings sweets to share under the mantra "Protein on Thursday, Carbs Tonight!"

We got a little mixed up one fall, though, when a local merchant asked if he could donate a turkey to the church. He and his family were first generation immigrants so our verbal communication was not always completely clear. In visiting with him about his gift, I was not sure if he was giving us a frozen turkey to give to a family in need or if he was giving us a prepared turkey to eat at church. Repeated attempts at clarification only made things murkier.

So, on Sunday morning I explained the situation to the congregation. They all chuckled and nodded their heads in recognition of occasional communication issues in the corner stores. I left them with the statement, "So, for church tonight, come hungry, but not too hungry."

Actually, coming to church hungry, but not too hungry, is a good guide for me every week.

Sometimes I come to church a little too full. On the weeks I've over-studied or under exercised I find myself not wanting to feast on the Word. I'm not really that open or receptive to other people's understandings, testimonies, or needs. A little hunger changes that completely.

Of course, if the week has been all about exercise and my Bible study time has been limited to the verses printed on bumper stickers affixed to the cars speeding past me on the freeway, then I come to church so hungry that the Word offered is more than I can handle, the same way that a person who is truly starving won't be healed by being dropped off at the all-you-can-eat buffet. I need to already have some food in the system if the available nutrients are going to give me strength, wholeness, and satisfaction.

If my spirit is to be healthy, I need to spend time digesting the meat of the Gospel throughout the week. That's not to say that Sundays should be without substance. Rather, there are things that I need to spend some lengthy, personal time on. I can't fit the deep mystery of God into a 40 minute sermon so I need time to chew on it and digest small bites at a time.

By the same token, I need to be in a group of the faithful to both speak and hear the testimonies of God in our world today. They give energy and invigorate for the tasks ahead. This kind of celebration (the icing on the cake?) can only really happen in a collective group. That's not to say my personal time with God should be without praise and celebration. Rather, the Spirit's promised presence when two or more are gathered in His name is something that can't be found in the same way when I'm alone.

If I don't get some good protein mid-week by chewing on the meat of the Gospel, I won't be ready for the carbs on Sunday when we celebrate God's goodness in our lives. And if I only get the carbs on Sunday then I'll crash mid-week when they're burned up in the work of the tasks God calls me to.

Protein on Thursday. Carbs Tonight.

Of course, that particular Sunday night before Thanksgiving we were delighted when, shortly before the service, the owner of the corner store pulled up to the church. His wife and another woman carried in a roaster with a giant steaming hot falling-off-the-bone delicious turkey for the congregation to eat.

Hungry, but not too hungry, we were able to share in the blessings of the Banquet together.

Lord, let me worship You in spirit and in truth. Help me to honor Your name.

GOODER

His friend came with him to church for the first time. My heart always gives a teen-aged boy a little extra credit when he brings an unchurched friend with him from off the street corners where they've been hangin'. Their coming in and sitting in the back together brought me delight.

Now, why they chose to come in with the old folks like me at a prayer meeting instead of one of the youth services baffled me. I wasn't sure if they would engage well with what was going on.

So we were all a bit surprised when, as one of the older ladies expressed a prayer concern, this new kid's hand shot up in the air. Though at church for the first time, he wanted to pray for her.

Granted, I'd given my standard spiel to the group earlier in the service reminding them that prayer was simply talking with God and that we need not be worried or scared about doing so publicly. People usually pay about as much attention to that as they do safety instructions on an airplane. I guess someone was listening that night.

And the kid believed me.

His direct, heartfelt, and insightful few sentences drew

to a close and he looked up at me with a "What do I do now?" expression on his face.

I said to him, "Amen?"

He grinned and said, "Amen."

And as he did, the boy who brought him opened his eyes and with a surprised look on his face pleasantly exclaimed, "He prays gooder than me!"

Like that kid, it's easy for me to be surprised when someone who is less experienced, less qualified, does something gooder than me.

I've been in church all my life. I've been to seminary and have a MA in Theology. I've been a pastor for a long time and have read and studied and prayed and served in many capacities. I have lots of experience and am qualified for the task --- just like the Pharisees and Sadducees and Scribes.

My training and experience are good, important, and beneficial so long as I don't forget that these temporal credentials are not qualifications in the Kingdom. An open and honest relationship with God, even if it's just begun after coming in off the street corner with your friend, is key.

And if I want to get gooder at what I do, then I need to remember to believe like that new kid did. Through his prayer we all knew he believed God was interested in hearing from him and was concerned about this stranger he was praying for. He believed that the exact words weren't as important as the fact that they were being said. He believed that he was as qualified as anyone else in the room to talk with God.

So on the days I get a little too much Pharisee in me I hope God brings someone by who, when they do something surprising to me, will cause me to delightfully exclaim, "They did that gooder than me!"

Amen?

Amen.

Lord, teach me to walk humbly before you.

SIGHT

No one was surprised, really, when it happened.

This kid had been one of our most faithful participants in church so we'd noticed that his old pair of glasses had been repaired time and time again. So when I picked him up at the end of camp, finding them in pieces in his hand was almost to be expected.

A couple of the camp staffers pulled me aside. They felt bad about his glasses situation and had taken up a collection from the other staff so we could restore his sight.

That really helped when I dropped him off at home. I was able to tell Mom that we were ready to replace what was left of his specs so she made the appointment and I gave them a ride to the optometrist. He got his prescription updated and we found some amazingly durable yet sufficiently cool frames. I'd received enough in the collection from camp to cover all the costs.

I took him a couple days later to pick them up. He was so happy to be able to see clearly again and bounced up the steps back into his house when I dropped him off.

I didn't see him at church that weekend. That was unusual but not unheard of.

But then he wasn't there the next weekend, or the weekend after that, or the weekend after that. This was the new pattern. I'd bump into him on the streets once in a while but church was clearly something he wasn't interested in.

It was somewhere in that time when I let those six dangerous words creep into my head:

After all we've done for you.

I don't know that I actually said them, but they were festering inside me. WE took him to camp. WE collected the money to get the new glasses. WE took him to the optometrist. WE paid the bill. WE gave him a ride.

Yet he wasn't hanging out with us anymore.

After all we'd done for him.

And when I find those thoughts and feelings inside me know I'm ready for a time out. Because when those words are in me I know I can be saying a lot of unsightly things.

Those words say that I have ulterior motives in ministry.

Those words say my love is conditional.

Those words say that I'm not serving, I'm exchanging.

Those words say that doing the right thing is only necessary when payback in imminent.

Those words shift my actions from "Thy will be done" to "My will be done."

Those words say that the most important thing is what I get out of serving, not what those who I serve get out of what I do.

I don't like what those words say about me. I don't like the kind of god those word's actions in me reflect to the world.

Because Jesus has done more for me that I could ever recognize much less pay back. And I trust that since He loves me unconditionally that He's not up there brooding over the thought, *After all I've done for him*.

So I when those words start creeping into my head it's time for a motivation check and an attitude adjustment. Why am I here? Why do I do what I do? What kind of invisible expectations have I placed on people? What must people do in order for me to love and serve them?

When I can get the right answers to those questions deep enough in my heart, my mind, body, and spirit, it starts showing in my attitude. It's then that I can really get back to serving others.

And months later, once my vision had been corrected in this case, the kid didn't owe me anything and I was free to love and serve him again.

Only then did he find his way back to the church.

Create in me a clean heart, Lord.

BOARDS

Fresh new boards covered the windows and doors of the house. The old boards had been there a long time.

I remember seeing this house when we were looking for a place to live in the neighborhood. It was boarded up then but still appeared in good condition. It's on the quietest street in our neighborhood. The houses on either side of it are in excellent condition. It's the only house on that block that I've ever seen boarded up. The owner was not interested in selling it back then and must not be willing to sell it now, either.

So there are fresh boards on the house. Though they're better than the old boards which had begun to rot, the house is still a board-up.

It's hard for me to understand why someone would keep a house boarded up for so long. They could live in it or rent it or sell it. Certainly there's something useful they could do with it rather than just reboard the windows and doors every couple of decades.

Then again, I do understand a bit about keeping some things boarded up.

I have places inside me that I don't want to deal with that I've kept boarded up for years. There are dark corners full of grime and pain and resentment and things I've completely forgotten about that I don't want to see. Even when I get a chance to go in and try to clean things out I prefer to instead put new boards up and move along to more pleasant areas.

And I want God to respect the boards, too. Yes, I know that the Spirit will bring new life to all areas I let Him in. But I've had Him work on so much of me that I know His remodeling projects can take a long time and are often painful. Though I am absolutely sure the results of His presence will bring life, I just don't want to deal with the process.

So guarding the boarded up doors becomes as important as the boards themselves.

There are no signs from the city on the house. Yet, for all practical purposes, even with the new boards this house is condemned. John 3:18 reminds us that I don't need to have someone spray paint the word "condemned" on the parts of my life where I lack trust in the Savior; that message is self-inflicted.

I fantasize that God would work like they do on the television remodeling shows. I could invite Him in, He'd send me to Disney World for a week, and then I could come back with all my old junk removed and a new life in front of me.

But He wants me to pick up a hammer, too, and take ownership of the process.

When I've done so in the past -- when I've taken down the boards and let Him remodel other areas of my life -- I've received nothing less than an abundance of joy and peace as a result.

So somewhere deep inside me there's a hope that I'll work up the courage and strength to remove the boards on those portions of my life that I haven't yet given completely to Him. Then, by His grace, we'll enter into the next episode in the story of my life's remodeling.

Let your mercy and grace flow, Lord. Let your light shine in my darkness and let me live in the fullness of Your presence.

TABLES

Even before kids arrived we knew there wouldn't be room for them. The young adults on a mission trip who were in charge of Bible School that August took up most of the space in the tiny storefront. We would need to move most of our activities to the park a block away.

The day before our festivities were to begin, we all walked down the sidewalk to scope out how to get the kids safely across the street and to determine where we would need to haul tables and chairs each day.

When we arrived we were pleasantly surprised to find several brand new heavy duty wooden picnic tables with attached benches. They were right under the trees where we were thinking of setting up our tables. They hadn't been there the day before. None of the neighbors noticed anyone delivering them and were just as surprised to see the tables as we were.

Bible School flew by. We had bunches of kids. Many of those kids were new to the congregation. The young adults on their mission trip led great lessons and activities. We even had one person find a grocer who provided lunch for all the kids each day. Those new tables got a good workout. They couldn't have been more perfect.

Though Bible School ended on Friday, the young

adults still had one day left in town. We decided to spend Saturday cleaning up an empty lot.

So it was early on Saturday morning when we noticed it. The tables were gone. No one, including the neighbors whose houses face the park, saw them removed. They somehow appeared in time for Bible School and vanished as soon as it was over.

We never saw signs of those tables again.

Lord, surprise me today with Your mercy and care and blessing. May I revel in Your mysterious ways while I witness of and delight in You.

CAUSE

The gold, low-riding, tricked out Cadillac pulled up in front of the school. Both front doors opened and two massive young men got out of the front seat simultaneously. Each was adorned in high-end gang apparel and a variety of gold jewelry. The tough anger on their faces caused everyone to pause.

One opened the back door of the car while the other reached his hand inside to assist the lady in exiting the vehicle.

She had a fresh hairdo and was dressed to the nines. As she emerged it was clear that both men were rendered helpless by the mesmerizing power she held over them.

The sheer delight on her face captivated the rest of us as she slowly walked into the school with one man on each arm. The man on her left let go only long enough to open the school door. He then took her frail hand as she laboriously navigated the step up and in.

As they waited with her in line to vote, she started a conversation with a couple of her friends who had gotten to the polls a few minutes before her. The two friends said they would wait for her afterward. With great dignity, they hobbled along with their canes toward a few chairs along the wall.

The three women sat together and visited quietly while keeping an eye out as to see who had made it to the polls. Just a glance into their eyes told quite a story.

For those eyes had seen lynchings. And those feet that now needed a cane had marched. The arms that had been supported to reach the polls had been linked together in solidarity in standing for justice. They'd sat at the lunch counters and in the front of the bus. They knew what fire hoses and police dogs and night sticks could do. That day they remembered what they had been through and marked some of the fruits of their sufferings.

The men who had driven her hadn't voted. They loitered in a corner. If they even hinted at being impatient or wanting get back to their other dealings, one brief look shot across the room from her put an immediate end to it.

When I look at my role in building His kingdom of righteousness, peace, and joy, I'd like to say that I'm like one of those elderly women. Truthfully, though, I must confess my solidarity is more often with the men who were with her.

I don't clearly see or understand or begin to appreciate the sacrifices and suffering that have made it possible to fulfill my calling in His work. Be it the saints of old or people who currently give beyond their means to make sure that I have a salary, it's often lost on me.

Plus I know that there are material and emotional benefits if I deal only in the portions of the Gospel that are the opiate of the masses rather than getting fully engaged in the cause of the Peaceable Kingdom. It's easier to surround myself with shiny possessions that show my status to others (though mostly to convince myself of my own worth) rather than to go through the hardships it takes to bring worth and dignity and justice to others.

And if I can't get my head and heart lined up around these things, how can I possibly even begin to pretend to understand the cross?

But once in a while I hear the Story again. And as I do I'm reminded that His work is not just something from the past or for the future but is for the here and now.

So I have a choice each day. I can treat Him with respect and honor. It may be a bit inconvenient and I might get impatient but for it I'll be blessed. Or, I can pay the price of joining with Him in the task of building His kingdom in the here and now. The cause is His. The choice is mine.

Your cause be mine, great Lord divine.
Your aim be my ambition.
--- Bryan Jeffery Leech

RED

I was relieved when he came into church that night wearing a new red shirt. I'd never seen him wear red before nor have I seen him in red since. I hadn't asked him to do so but it was exactly what he needed to wear.

Turn the clock back about two and a half hours when a kid sitting on the floor of the church yelled, "Ouch!"

I went over to the kid to see what was wrong.

"It's hot!" he said, pointing to the font.

It was the first time I'd used the heater on the font and was unsure of exactly how well it worked. Now the steel sides of the horse trough we used for baptisms were painfully hot to the touch.

This was not good.

So, we unplugged the heater and removed the table we'd used as a lid in hopes that the water would cool before the service.

Only then did we learn that the tabletop has once been painted red. The steamy water had leached all the pigments out of it.

Yes, that's right. We had bright red scalding hot water

in the font with no way to drain and refill it in time for the service.

So during the short time remaining I did all I could think to do. I opened the front door to let the January air into the building in hopes of cooling things down. I set my sermon aside and frantically flipped through the Bible seeing if I could somehow have a message that involved either the Red Sea or being "baptized in the blood" or both.

But with his coming to church in a red shirt and the water cooling off to that of bathwater I was able to switch back to the sermon I had prepared in advance.

During that message each person was given a hard, crumbling piece of clay. They then got to quickly dip their clay into a bowl of water and continue working with it. The newly pliable clay was now able to be shaped and molded into something it couldn't have been before.

I remembered my own baptism and my commitment to letting the Potter mold this clay into something He wants. And I thought of my unnecessarily frantic state that afternoon as I had tried to make up for my own ignorance and error.

I realized (for the millionth time) that He still had a lot of molding to do and that I needed to step back and let Him reshape me to serve peacefully in the circumstances where I find myself.

Be it the parting of the Red Sea or a baptism candidate in a red tee, God continues to use the strangest of circumstances in forming his people into a growing vessel for faith and trust. May the waters of my baptism continue to soak in deeply that I might be easily shaped in His hands.

Melt me. Mold me. Fill me. Use me.
Spirit of the Living God, fall afresh on me.
                      --- Daniel Iverson

JOURNEY

His South Carolina accent told me he wasn't from around here even before he informed me of such. He had missed his south-bound bus home and was looking for a way to get back on the road. He hadn't eaten for a couple of days, either.

After he devoured the warmed-up can of ravioli I'd microwaved, he asked if I could give him the small amount of money needed to change his bus ticket to the one leaving later that night. Cash is something I know enough not to do, so I came up with some other viable options for him.

I offered to go to the bus station to change the ticket and pay small amount with my credit card to get him home.

That was not acceptable to him because he said it was asking too much of me.

I offered to connect him with some emergency services that would help him get home.

That was not acceptable to him because he said those services were for people with much bigger problems than his.

I offered to help him contact relatives in South Carolina so they could get him a ticket.

That was not acceptable to him because he said it would create too much work and bother for them.

I returned to my first offer and directed him to my van so he and I could drive the few blocks back to the bus station where he could catch his bus.

That was not acceptable to him. He had a solution in mind, that being him receiving a few dollars so he could change the ticket himself. Nothing else would be acceptable.

I asked him if he wanted to go back to South Carolina.

"Yes!" he said, exasperated and a bit angry that I couldn't seem to grasp this basic concept. I reviewed his options.

He came back with a plan for me to go to an ATM to get money to give him so he could change his ticket.

I said no. He started crying.

"I just want to get home. I just need to get home!"

He then got up, walked out of the church, and disappeared into the night.

Over the next couple of days I saw him walking the streets, despondent, angry, frustrated, and clutching an expired bus ticket in his left hand.

I wish I knew how to not be like this guy. I don't always know how to take help from people or from God, especially if I've been traveling alone for a while. I can spend so much time and energy designing plans and solutions that I limit the range of what help is acceptable. I can only see one possible way home.

And when my plans were generated in a state of hunger, especially in emotional or spiritual hunger, warmed-up canned responses from those around me don't offer enough strength and clarity for me to see any differently.

I know that being open to plans beyond what I can conceive is where I can experience miraculous grace. I mean, if Moses had spend his whole day demanding that God build a bridge he would not have heard the call to raise his staff and have an unexpected path home open up for him and his people.

But knowing and acting on that knowledge are two different things. Trust is a key element in moving to action. When I'm feeling out of place in a world that's unresponsive to my solutions, my ability to trust falls. My blinders make me blind.

What if I had spent a few more minutes with the South Carolinian man, empathizing with his emotions and state of mind rather that jumping straight to alternative solutions? Maybe we both could have realized that his unstated goal was to find some dignity and worth. He might have been more open to plans different than his own that would have taken him home had we spent some time developing basic trust.

Perhaps if I can recognize when I'm fixated on a single solution that I need to listen and trust God and those He has placed in my path. I have to remember that He wants me to get me back to the journey He's sent me on and that He has a way beyond what I can see.

Lord, remind me that my thoughts are not Your thoughts and my ways are not Your ways. Let me journey in trust.

COATS

"Just take these," she said as she hoisted four men's coats into my hands. She had turned her head, seeming both to not want to watch as she let go of the garments and not wanting me to notice the puffiness of her eyes that were holding back the remaining tears.

I knew the coats had come at a great cost. I had seen them before. They had been hanging in her house right where her husband had left them. In the years since his passing their presence had reminded her of his presence, mementos of the blessing she'd lost.

But cold came early that fall. And when she saw the cardboard sign being held by the shivering hands of a homeless man she knew was my friend she had to do something.

The moment when grief for what was lost is overtaken by grief for those who never had something to begin with puts us in a position of challenge. And when we boldly, painfully choose to respond by taking the blessings from our past and using them to heal the present the Spirit can't seem to help but move.

I took those coats to four very different men: tall, short, stout, lean. I said to each, "I don't know if this will fit; it might be too _____ (short, long, small, bulky) but try it on and we'll see."

And though these men would need to shop in different sections of stores to find well-fitting clothing, each coat appeared as if custom tailored for that individual.

Warm memories of blessings past, baptized by tears, transformed into blessings of warmth against today's cold winds.

Lord, help me know Your presence in all attempts to serve You.

WHISTLE

"You need to talk to him NOW and make his stop yelling cat calls and whistling at women out the front door of the church."

Such was the greeting that began my Sunday morning.

I set aside the sermon notes and put the prayers on hold so I could have a talk with him. The talk included the requested directives.

From there we had a discussion about why this behavior was bad. The top two reasons were 1.) it had the opposite effect on the women he was interested in; and 2.) it made the church look bad in a scary way.

Since I had a captive audience and knew I wouldn't get to that last review of my sermon notes anyway, he and I spent some time coming up with better plans. We thought of ways he might be able to make himself more attractive to women. These included being kind and respectful to all women, whether he was particularly interested in them or not, and to work on being friends with people rather than simply seeking out physical relationships.

It was a good talk, at least for me. I needed to hear it

because of the way I sometimes approach trying to attract people to the church.

Sometimes the people I'm most interested in as potential church members are people who come with lots of skills, lots of energy, and who already have their lives put together pretty well. Leadership potential is especially hot.

I've come to learn, though, that many of the popular methods used by churches today aren't very effective in reaching them. Even methods that seem kind and loving "on paper" seem manipulative to the person on the receiving end. These methods and strategies often have the opposite effect of what was intended and make the church look bad in a scary kind of way.

Jesus showed kindness and respect to all people no matter who they were. He became known as a friend of "sinners" while still being invited to dinner at the home of "respectable" people. He built friendships with and provided ministry to people who would become disciples as well as those who would betray Him.

Some people came to see Jesus just for the show or the healing or the free bread and fish. But some received much more than they expected and then used what they had been given as raw materials for building God's Kingdom.

Evangelism, like human love, has its ups and downs and twists and turns. It has no guarantees. Perhaps if I became more motivated by Jesus' love than my personal desires for people to join the church, some might respond out of dignity and curiosity rather than being repelled by my bad behavior.

Be they Zealots or tax collectors or fishermen, lifelong disciples or here just for the show or healing or free bread, all are loved by a God who is calling their names. May I help them hear that calling rather than drown it out with my own whistle.

Jesus, help me see as You see, serve as You serve, love as You love.

SWARM

The four fly strips were completely full.

Completely.

That scene was truly disgusting but only amplified by the fact that we had hung them just twenty minutes earlier.

Some mysterious thing had caused an infestation of flies that filled the entire church building that Saturday. It was how I pictured Egypt at the time of the plagues and I was hoping that the frogs would be arriving soon to help us.

We'd tried swatting them. We'd tried spray. We'd tried fly strips. We'd tried everything they'd recommended at the corner store. We'd had prayer and binding and loosing and casting out. The flies still seemed to have the upper hand.

Having run out of ideas, we set off enough insecticide bombs to kill the house plants and went home for the night.

The next morning we quite literally swept the layer of flies off the floor of the church and wiped the insecticide off the chairs as we set up for the first service.

Things seemed to go reasonably well, but by the third service we were in trouble. A cloud of flies had assembled and taken over the back room. They were loud enough that we could hear them over the speaker. They were starting to spill out into the main room and were hovering a few feet over the worshippers seated for the sermon.

We cut to the closing song.

And on the last verse the flies had their final say as one flew into my mouth. Naturally, it got stuck on my soft palate so it would neither come out nor go in. The song ended with me trapped in front of the congregation trying to scoop a still living fly out of the back of my mouth.

Yes, it was quite a Sunday.

Did I mention that it was Easter?

The invitations. The decorations. The new families. The guest ministers. The special crafts. The really great experiences we had (at least in the first 2 1/2 services). The willingness of people to endure swarms of flies.

I didn't mention those things either, did I?

It seems often the case that I spend most of my days battling swarms – physical, psychological, emotional, spiritual – that seem to take over. I pray at them, spray at them, or try to get them to stick to something (or someone) else. Sometimes when I take my eyes off them and try instead lift my voice in praise they choke me off.

And though I might want to just call it in early, it's Easter. I have a living Savior. And if I can close my mouth and look hard through the swarm there are signs of resurrection happening amid the frantic buzz.

Because the swarms are real and so is the One who calls me through them. Focusing on the flies leads to the despairing life of a losing battle as I try to completely rid myself of them. Denying them as a means of focusing on the Christ will eventually choke off my sharing of the Good News with others.

The flies died off a few days later; we never found out why or how they got there. But because of Easter, He is still with us and will be, through swarms or clear skies, even unto the ends of the earth.

Lord, You are the Eternal One. Thank you.

FUMES

With the unbridled energy of an 8-year-old, he burst through the door of the church and happily exclaimed, "Dad! Dad! There are firemen in our HOUSE!"

I did not greet the news with the same enthusiasm.

I stuck my head outside and saw that there were red flashing lights on my block. We postponed the church service for a few minutes so I could run home to find out what exactly was happening.

The firemen had come into our house after a neighbor two doors down had been taken to the hospital with carbon monoxide poisoning. The source of the problem was a broken water heater in her basement.

Because all of our houses on the block are connected, the firemen wanted to check our CO levels just to be safe. Some of the invisible, odorless, toxic gas had silently seeped through their walls, through another neighbor's house, then through our walls.

The firemen had gone into our basement. With all my junk piled up down there I was relieved that they didn't cite us for a fire hazard. Instead, they found the CO levels elevated to slightly higher than normal. Their prescription was to open the basement windows for an hour or so to let some fresh air in.

Some days I find myself especially lethargic --- physically, emotionally, spiritually, mentally, or any combination of the above. It's really easy for me to succumb to it and let myself drift off.

But I've learned that I often get this way because of something broken in the basement of someone else's life. Addiction, emergency assistance, disease in our broken health care system, hunger, mental breakdowns, substandard housing, school safety, and the litany of other daily activities in da 'hood lead to dark places in peoples' lives.

Through both geography and ministry, our lives become interconnected. And though we keep healthy boundaries, the toxins in their lives can silently seep into mine.

Without noticing, I can get completely overcome, especially if I let those toxins build up in the part of my life where I keep all my own junk. All my issues combined with theirs can make my own life quite hazardous.

That's why it's so important for me to keep a window open. If I'm all sealed up inside, the fresh Air cannot come in and restore me.

Sometimes He sends his refreshing breezes through Scripture or prayer or song or some of the expected ways. Other times it's through less spiritual things like a good nap or a funny television show. In any case, keeping open to Him in all of His ways is the prescription to restoring health.

Because the Spirit is like the wind that blows wherever it wants to (John 3:8) and it's my job to keep the window open to let His freshness restore my soul.

Lord, restore my soul and lead me on paths of righteousness for Your name's sake.

NOT

When I first heard the call to step out on the streets in ministry God and I had a lot of conversations about it.

One of us was calm. The other one was me.

I remember one of the conversations quite distinctly. In it, I panic-strickenly listed all the things I was afraid of. I had come up with an exhaustive list that I found quite impressive.

It wasn't so much what He said in His typically brief reply but the way He said it.

Fear NOT.

It was the same reply given so many times in the scriptures. But this time it was different. In my mind I've always translated that statement into "Do not be afraid." That may be accurate from the Hebrew and Greek, but getting me to dismiss my fears didn't seem to be His goal.

Wrapped up in those two words was a new translation which sounded more like this:

Fear NOT stepping out.
Fear NOT heeding the call.
Fear NOT going places that scare you.
Fear NOT doing this.

And it wasn't about eternal salvation or worldly punishment or somehow losing out on God's love; that is way outside the nature of God and would have just reflected even more of my personal insecurities.

Instead it was more a call to recognizing that the safe, clean, predictable, stable world I had built was, in reality, a much scarier place than the full, deep, rich, abundant land that He's promised.

He never discounted my impressive list of fears. In fact, as the conversation wound down I felt like if I had not recognized the very real fears it would have been a bigger problem than my listing them for Him.

The earth-sized fears I could see were real. The heaven-sized *Fear NOT* provided a counterbalance.

And strangely, in that tension between fear and Fear NOT I found peace. It seems to me counterintuitive, but there it was ---- that peace that passes understanding.

Yes, in our conversations One was calm. By the end, the other was moving that way.

Grant us wisdom, grant us courage,
Lest we miss Thy kingdom's goal.
                              --- Harry E. Fosdick

GREAT

Some places call it "Prayer and Testimony" and no one comes. We call it "Open Mike" and people get excited about the opportunity.

And he was excited as he came up the front of the church that Sunday morning after Christmas.

"This was the best Christmas EVER!" he exclaimed. He then told of not even wanting gifts and instead taking the money he was given and buying candy for the neighbor kids. He talked about how great it was to be looking for ways to help people instead of just wanting more things.

He ended with, "And up until a couple of weeks ago I'd never even been in a church before. This stuff is GREAT!"

He laughed out loud all the way back to his seat and we celebrated by joining him in laughter and applause.

For me it's easy to forget that this stuff is GREAT. The daily grind of preparing for and cleaning up after church activities, the constant pressing needs of the community, the seeming hopelessness of the conditions in the neighborhood, all on top of my own unresolved issues clutters the manger so much that it's sometimes hard to see the Baby.

But when someone comes in and sees Jesus for the first time, the clutter gets pushed out of the way and I, too, can stand in awe of Him and the greatness of His ways.

And when I can, my life again becomes its own "Open Mike" in the world as the Joy, Hope, Love, and Peace of the Gospel are lived out loud.

Lord, let me delight in You always.

THWAP

Thwap!

We all heard it and knew what it meant.

A couple people glanced around to see who would respond but she and I already had sufficient adrenaline in us. We had jumped up from our chairs and were now heading toward the thwap.

Prayer meeting would have to wait.

As we turned on the lights in the storage room we could see the rat in the trap.

"It's still alive!" she yelled as the rat and trap dragged themselves across the carpet. "Give me a pipe."

A little scared (of her, not the rat) I handed over an old piece of pipe that was by the door. She took it and immediately began bludgeoning the creature.

It tried to escape but it was no match to her passion. The blood-stained wall and the new markings on the carpet now warned future predators of her victory.

Two latex gloves and one plastic bag later, I disposed of the corpse while she reset the trap.

Prayer meeting resumed.

When I'm trying to exterminate things that make my life miserable, like my issues and ego and habits and insecurities (read: sin) I want someone like this woman on the journey with me.

I need people to pray with me. But once in a while when the time is right, I need someone to courageously march into the dark rooms inside me where I store my old stuff, turn on some light, and take a blunt object to the problem.

Though it's messy and uncomfortable, it's important.

Because I remember years ago the letter from my pastor that contained the direct correction I needed. And I remember the annoyingly persistent accountability from a fellow disciple during a time of rapid personal growth. And I remember the counselor finally saying, "Just get over it." Those things helped free me and helped me grow more than closing our eyes and praying harder would have.

Each of those people had a choice. They could have let fear of damaging our relationships get in the way of what needed to be done and glanced around hoping for someone else to do the job. But they knew that out of relationships based on solid faith, prayer, and mutual respect come opportunities to engage in passionate, scary, dangerous, painful conflict that can ultimately lead to a more whole self.

And though our relationship may get a little stained and bloodied at first, I have to trust that His grace will sustain us and open the possibility for even deeper friendship as a result.

It's then that we are truly free to resume our prayers before our Maker together.

Lord, help me hear, know, and respond well to Truth.

IMPORTANT

The kids were getting squirrely. Through their participation in church they had earned a trip to a local restaurant for ice cream sundaes.

Vanilla
Chocolate
Whipped Cream
Sprinkles
Hot Fudge
Cherries

Though these items were all clearly on the menu, all we'd been given so far were glasses of water. We'd been seated for nearly an hour.

The wait staff had been running around the restaurant and seeming to work. Yet, when we looked around, we noticed no one else in the restaurant had ice cream, either. Meanwhile, the line at the entrance grew longer and longer, winding out the door and into the night.

Our ability to entertain our kids had maxed out quite a bit earlier so I flagged down the manager to get an update on our order. He let us know that their computer system had gone down and they were all working on it. "Once it's fixed we'll be able to fill your order," he said.

Getting desperate, I looked at him and said, "I know that the computer system is really important to you, but as a customer, I don't care. It doesn't take a computer to put ice cream in a bowl."

He looked shocked. He then went over to the computer station and had all the wait staff start scooping ice cream and distributing desserts to the customers. As we were fed, the computer healed.

As a pastor it's easy for me to be like the manager of that restaurant. The things needed to make the church run smoothly don't always like me too much. It seems that if the video projector is working then the sound system refuses to do so. The box of scissors goes rogue at craft time and there aren't enough green crayons to go around. The Popsicles leak all over the freezer and turn everything in it blue. And the package I thought was toilet paper was actually paper towels and we're now Charmin-free with a line of little kids at the bathroom.

And that's before we even begin to talk about the all-consuming denominational issues, interpersonal conflicts, theological hot spots, spiritual authority questions, and meetings upon meetings upon meetings.

But none of these things are on the list of why people come through the door of the church.

Healing
Hope
Repentance
Strength
Encouragement
Wisdom
Prayer
Community
Praise
Fellowship

These are the things people seek. Though the background organizing is important to make sure the doors stay open and the big issues of the day will eventually impact how we deliver the Message, I need to make sure I focus my energy, and everyone else's, too, on helping people get what they so desperately need that they found their way to the church's doors.

Because Jesus didn't say that he came so we could be organized and have all the answered nailed down. The Pharisees and Sadducees already had a corner on that market. He said that He came that we could have life, full and abundant (John 10:10).

And creation is getting more than just a little squirrely; it groans for the liberating truth of the Gospel.

May I not focus so much on the church's internal workings and, instead, serve those who have come so that they might dine at the Table and not be left standing out in the dark.

Lord, be my vision.

WHATEVER

Brown construction paper.

That, plus some well-worn crayons and dull scissors, composed the entire allotment of our craft supplies.

And for I-don't-know-how-many weeks in a row, whenever the kids came to church, craft time meant making things out of brown construction paper.

We'd scoured the Bible looking for stories we could share with the kids in which a corresponding craft could be based on brown construction paper:

-Crosses
-Loaves and Fishes
-10 Commandments tablets
-Boats for Peter to step out of
-Bricks for the Tower of Babel
-Balaam's Donkey
-Rocks (as in "He who is without sin may cast the first stone")

As the list grew so did the desperation.

Walking to the church that chilly, gray Sunday afternoon, brown construction paper was all I had. I had no lesson. I had no activity. I had no idea what to do with the paper or the kids and no energy left to even try to figure anything out.

I'd like to say that I prayed for wisdom or inspiration or for a miracle or a combination thereof but I was too drained for that. It was a more of a half-hearted "Whatever" kind of prayer instead.

I arrived at the church just as one of our volunteers was pulling up in her car. She beeped the horn and flagged me over.

As I crossed the street she hopped out of her car and said, "My mom was in town and we were at the warehouse club yesterday. She asked if she could buy some things for the church."

As she said this the trunk popped open revealing its contents. In it were stacks of construction paper of every possible color. There were buckets of magic markers and containers of scissors. Yarn. Tape. Clay. Glue (both bottles and sticks!). The smell of the fresh boxes of crayons was the sweetest perfume.

This was Noah's rainbow and Joseph's coat of many colors and the lilies of the field and Lydia's purple goods all stuffed in a Nissan Sentra. We emptied the trunk and set the supplies on the table for all the kids to see.

And they reveled in the color. Busy hands drew and

colored and folded and cut. Boisterous voices and laughter joined the celebration.

Today there was no hunting and hording and fighting over the best crayons. Instead, the bounty shared with us begot a sharing of this bounty with one another.

Today's craft:

Thank You Cards.

Whatever, Lord. Whatever.

DRUM

He gave the church his drum at the end of the service as a way of thanking us for the ministry he received that day.

He and his drum had staggered in to the church about 15 minutes before it was time to start. After visiting with me, he stumbled to the chairs and sat his drunken self down right in the middle of the room.

He played the drum during every song we sang. His rhythms were his own and had absolutely nothing to do with the songs the rest of the people were trying to sing.

During the quiet times and while I was preaching, he occasionally moaned, cried a little, and slurred a few words. These were usually accompanied by some random drumbeats.

All of this was to the complete dissatisfaction of those who had gathered that morning.

Once he presented the gift and left, a few people came to express their frustrations about what had just happened. Their concerns were legitimate and well-justified; it was a challenging hour for us all.

Then I relayed the conversation he and I had before the service.

Earlier that week he had been walking up the block by the church. A car had sped around the corner. It missed him but hit and killed a girl who was on her way home from school. That day was fresh in all our minds, too.

In trying to deal with what he'd experienced he had come back to the scene that morning. He'd found the discarded toy drum along the way and had used it to keep his hands busy and accent his emotions.

As he left that corner he found himself standing in front of the church and he believed that God had put it there just for him that day.

We didn't have much we could do for him in the way of skills and resources. We couldn't fix his problems. But having a place to sit, to cry, to express himself, and to think about life itself was the ministry most needed that day.

And it's the kind of ministry I need sometimes, too.

I'm not always ready to have all my problems fixed and if people try to do so they just make things worse. I don't always need skills and resources used on me. Sometimes I just need to sit with a group of people who will let me think and make random expressions to try to process where I am.

Because life gets intense --- intensely troubling and

intensely joyful. And intense times call for a decompression that can only come in the presence of others and the Other.

So when you see me getting ready to beat my drum again and you know it's not in sync with what's happening around me, I beg a bit more grace than usual for a few minutes.

And I'll work at not trying to fix you when you need to bang things out now and again, too.

Then when we're done we can give those drums back to Him as we return into the intensity life can bring.

Let the Comforter be among us, Lord.

CELEBRATE

"Well, Happy Birthday!" I said to him and his mom. I was standing by their crowded front steps gathering information and filling in the "Date of Birth" blank on his camp form when I realized that it was his holiday.

After wishing him well I tried to move on to the next question. I was not successful.

The man who was also sitting on their steps dealing drugs called into the house to his associates. He announced that it was the boy's birthday and they all got excited. They came to the steps, greeted him boisterously, gave him big hugs, and each handed him cash.

The party spread to the stoop next door and those nearby all came over for the celebration. More gave money. Another flagged down the ice cream truck and got him a treat.

After a few minutes I could see that the spontaneous party was just getting started and that there was no use in trying to finish the camp forms that night. I headed to the next camper's house knowing I would have to get the other mundane information later.

I was frustrated to not have the forms done. The deadline for their submission was looming and it was hard to find his mom at home, much less lucent. Who knew if I would even be able to get this taken care of?

These are the kinds of moments that I'm reminded just how much of a Pharisee I can be. Of all the people on the steps that night, I'm the one who publicly preached about Joy, Hope, Love, and Peace yet was totally unprepared to celebrate a birthday. Gifts, food, and accolades seemed to pour out of nowhere from among all the others. The only thing I could focus on was the line that said, "Emergency Contact Information."

Don't get me wrong. What I was doing was important and necessary. But I thought it trumped the moment of celebrating the importance of this kid.

When I read the Gospels again, I see how Jesus got in trouble (with the Pharisees and Martha and the disciples and others) because he was ready and able to celebrate the goodness he found, even with those pesky tax collectors.

And if I were that kid, I would have seen both a group of people who were ready to drop everything to celebrate me and a person who only seemed interested in information about me. With whom would I have cast my allegiance?

So it's not surprising, really, that 12 years later he's taken over for the men who once sat on his front steps. Oh, we still visit and he has good memories of activities at church and of his week at camp. They are simply distant memories that he was able to share with the ones who he felt loved him the most.

Lord, let love be my only debt.

OPEN

I kept the front door open while I was doing some work at the church. I let in some fresh air and hoped people would stop by and visit. So he felt quite comfortable when he came in to just pull up a chair and chat.

Him, "Let me ask you a question."

Me, "Sure."

H - You and your wife (Pause) you're (Pause) married?

M – Yes

H - And you have a child together, right?

M - Yep.

(Pause)

H - and he was born (Pause) *AFTER* you were married?

M - That's right.

(Pause)

H - Well, who else do you have a child by?

M - No one else. Just her.

(Pause)

H - Well who else does she have a child by?

M - No one.

After another long pause and a perplexed look on his face, he continued this line of questioning.

This went on for about 45 minutes with more pauses for him to think and more perplexed facial expressions with each answer given.

In the middle of one line of questions he stood up, looked at me, shook his head, and without saying anything else wandered out into the night. My life was too much for him to handle and he just had to leave.

Sometimes I have to put the Bible down and walk away into my own night, too. There are things in the text that I've reviewed and studied and wrestled with. I've had long talks with God about them but mostly I just shake my head. After a while, though, I have to recognize that God's way of thinking is just so very different from mine and, from where I sit, it's just too much for me to handle.

It wasn't long after that evening's open door

conversation that he and his mom moved across town and we lost track of each other.

So it was a real surprise when I parked my van in front of my house one Saturday afternoon about eight years later that I saw him riding his bike up my street.

"Remember me?" he asked as he pulled up beside me. I knew his face immediately and his name just a minute later. I asked what was going on in his life.

"I have a kid," he said. He grinned and held up his left hand as he said, "The mom and me, we're married." A gold band on his finger shown in the sunlight.

I don't know if those two conversations, eight years apart, had that much to do with each other. But the two together give me hope: not only hope for that kid and his family but hope for me, too.

Because it makes me wonder about my desire to better know the mind of God and the conversations and studies I've had to walk away from. I hope that they might be silently working in me and showing up in my life years later in ways I might not even remember or recognize.

And maybe when I run across those passages of scripture again they won't be quite as far out of my thought stream as when they first perplexed me.

Maybe stepping away let them quietly work into the fibers of my being without me even really noticing.

Maybe not.

But there is hope.

Thank you, Lord, for not ever giving up on me.

EVEN

He'd listened to the message attentively enough to have a question for me afterward. That always does my heart some good.

His question?

"Do you mean that *even I* can get baptized?"

Yes. That was the heart of the message. God loves all of us, offers forgiveness to all of us, and invites us all to the waters of baptism in sacramental relationship with Him. Through it he could fully become a member of the church.

That was a question that my middle-class self had never really pondered.

Even I?

I come from a world where opportunity abounds. I come from a world where inclusion is expected and that I have a *right* to belong. In my world I expect to have a variety of choices of groups who all would (or *should*) want me to be a member.

And in my world sin seems to have limitations. We describe our sinful state with terms like "issues" or "things I struggle with" or "personal weaknesses." Our past behaviors are referred to "youthful indiscretions" or "lapses in judgment." If many people like me are enmeshed in a particular sin, ranging from racism to "fudging" on our taxes, we say something like "that's just how things are" or "that's what everyone does."

My middle class world also has the resources to cover up or deal with our oft unnamed sin. We have financial resources that pay for rehab or cut a child support check each month. We have educational and emotional and family resources that help us navigate through sin-induced crises. We have social resources with polite company that help keep skeletons safely in our closets.

But he didn't have any of these things. His sin had been lived out publicly and had cost him dearly. There was no glossing over them and no one to pick up the pieces. He bore the scars and carried the stigma.

Plus, his was not a world full of opportunity. It was a world where exclusion was the norm and any hopes of inclusion had been dead so long that he didn't really remember that they even existed. He never felt that any group had ever wanted *him* to be a member.

So to be invited, to be welcome, to be included was radical. The hope of forgiveness was true liberation.

This makes me wonder how even I could have been baptized. With my privileged birthright and social safety net, with help in the waiting for my next crisis and my (if I were willing to admit to them) skeletons in my closet, could I have even begun to grasp the magnitude of this sacrament?

Even I?

If I were attentive to my own and my social class's sinfulness, might I be more able to fully engage in the radical liberation of the Christ?

That would really do my heart some good.

Lord, free me from the things that keep me captive.

BILL

The gas & electric bill came late in the day on Thursday. It was the first power bill we received since the expansion of our building so we were anticipating a big jump in how much we would owe. We had, in fact, budgeted for a ten-fold increase.

Even with that preparation I was still more than a little surprised. The bill was 40X (yes, *forty* times) the previous month's bill. In fact, this power bill was higher than our typical monthly offering receipts.

Dilemma.

This bill was too big for any specific prayer I knew. "Well, what are *YOU* going to do about *THIS*?" was about all I could offer.

I then started looking for His answer in all the typical places.

I called folks who had supervisory capacity over the ministry. They agreed it was a problem and told me to solve it.

The next day I called the power company to find out payment options. Their option was to pay it or have the gas and electric turned off.

I then did the math to see how much I could make at

a part time job. That's when I realized that even if I worked full time as a cashier at Target I would not make half as much as the power company wanted each month.

What to do?

You can call it denial. You can call it faith. You can call it shock. You can call it whatever you want, but the fact of the matter was that the problem was just way too big for me to do anything about that day. Since I didn't see Him doing anything in particular, I decided to get a good night's sleep and continue with the things I had scheduled for Saturday and Sunday.

When I got home from Saturday afternoon's meetings I found an envelope in the mail from some acquaintances in another city. We hadn't corresponded in a very long time and I found it odd that, since they'd never been to the church, the envelope bore its address.

Inside was a note saying they'd been thinking of our congregation this week and felt led to help in some way. The check was *twice* the amount of the power bill.

Wow.

The money and the hope that came with it carried us for a couple of months, at which point we discovered that the power company hadn't read our gas and electric meters; they had simply estimated what they thought we would use.

When they came out and actually read the meters they adjusted our balance accordingly.

Our bill read $0000.00 for the next four months.

I liked His solution just fine.

Show yourself strong, Lord, in my life and in the world around me.

PICKED

High school football was the topic of discussion. Many schools in the inner city don't field teams. Some of the ones that do have limited resources, both in finance and skill, to do things as well as their suburban counterparts.

The high school many of our kids attend is fortunate enough to have a team. So with several of our boys quite eager to play pick-up games each weekend in the park, I asked why they didn't join their school's team.

They all laughed.

"Pastor, the kids on our school's team are, you know, it's like in gym when you're making teams and they look like the ones that don't ever get picked."

I must confess that when I look over our little inner-city congregation it sometimes seems like I could accurately describe us that way, too.

Many of our folks have spent their whole lives not getting picked for the team.

Any team.

So it's easy when I see the abundant skill and financial resources of the Willow Creeks and

Saddlebacks of the world, much less the glitz and allure of the secular world's ways, to get depressed over how we can hardly suit up and therefore should plan for defeat.

But then I remember Gideon. And David. And Moses, Peter, James and John. Rahab. Ruth. The list goes on.

Who would have picked them, at least at the beginning of the story?

And I see the strength and courage and passion of our folks who dare to dream of the Kingdom. They're painfully aware of their resource restrictions but are just crazy enough to think they will impact this world for His glory.

It's true that the world might never pick us. On my better days I'm OK with that. I'll just keep on trying to keep us all in training and ready to run onto the field each time He calls our names.

Here am I, send me.

TOXINS

Our eyes filled with tears.

I'd like to say that it was because we'd gotten emotional over a movement in the Spirit, but that would not be accurate.

It was the fumes.

I don't remember the exact cause, but somehow the church was filled with gas from the sewer. It wasn't just a bad smell; the stinging toxins caused us all to react physically. We were quite certain that if someone had caused a spark the whole thing would have ended in a fiery bang.

Turning on the exhaust fans didn't help. Opening all the doors and windows didn't help. Stepping out of the building and breathing deeply ---- that helped.

Of course, this problem didn't exist at all on Saturday evening. I guess that's OK as we wouldn't have been able to pay the emergency fees to get someone out on the weekend to fix it anyway.

So we scoped out our options, gathered some old folding chairs, carried them to the nearby park, and set them up under the shade of a tree. We found some batteries for a boom box and pulled out some CDs to play. We posted a kid at the front door of the building and had him point the gathering parishioners to our new location.

Someone had thrown one of those big orange traffic barrels (the kind with the flashing light on it that road crews use in construction zones) into the park. Its flasher was no longer working so I set my Bible on it and used it as the day's pulpit.

Since we were just rolling with the punches, those who came planning to be indoors just rolled with things, too. Expectations for the day went down as everyone fumbled around a little bit, but in the end things turned out OK. We even had a couple of people who were in the park stop by to see what we were doing.

We called in the pros the first of the week and got the problem of the toxic gas solved.

Ever since that time I've become a little more sensitive to toxic fumes inside the church.

Interpersonal conflicts, programming debates, inflated egos, people not meeting each others' expectations, theological disagreements ---- the list goes on. These fumes can build up overnight in a church and have us all on the verge of tears.

And it seems like one spark will cause the whole thing to end in a fiery bang.

When this happens it's critical that we get some fresh Air. Open the windows and doors. Turn on the fans. And when that's not enough, we need to get someplace --- physically, spiritually, emotionally --- where our expectations of each other can be relaxed and where we can let the Spirit breathe.

For it's in those airy places where we can let our flashpoints dim and replace them with steady light from the Word.

Once we're breathing again we need to be humble enough to ask for help from others. Hoping the fumes will simply dissipate by themselves will just keep us in the same crisis.

And though not all the sources of toxins in a church can be repaired with one service call, we know through the cross that the price has already been paid and that restoration is on its way.

Breathe on me breath of God.

CHALK

The first warm and sunny Sunday after a cold bleak winter called us to have our kids' activities outdoors. With hope in their hearts and chalk in their hands they tumbled out into the fresh air to decorate the sidewalk with the bright colors of spring.

The kids were already at work when I stepped out the front door. They took turns striking poses and tracing each other as they lay on the concrete.

Within minutes, the kids proclaimed that they were finished. I looked on horrified to see the unadorned chalk outlines of a dozen children lining the sidewalk of the church. Some police tape would have made the scene complete.

They were puzzled as to why my face was contorted and why I didn't think they were finished. Not wanting to point out that it looked like the remnants of a massacre, I made a declaration.

"LOOK at these children on the sidewalk. NONE of them are wearing any CLOTHES! I don't allow naked children in front of this church so put some clothes on them right now!"

For a moment they were shocked. Then embarrassment kicked in as they took the many colors of chalk and created the latest fashions within the outlines. They added some jewelry and other essential bling before going inside to wash their hands. The faces, both on the sidewalk and on the kids themselves, carried smiles.

When I've come out of the bleak winter seasons in my soul there's often little more than what feels like a chalk outline of me left. And the start of a period of new growth can look more like a crime scene than a glorious new season.

But as I find my robes of righteousness, don my helmet of salvation, buckle my belt of truth, walk around in my shoes of peace, and add the essential bling of a polished shield of faith, I move from a remnant of the past season to joy-filled life in Him.

Because when Spring arrives in the soul again, it's time to get out and revel in the fresh Air.

Lord, you are the restorer of my soul.

SUPPLIED

Like so many women that day, she took the little girl's hand and helped her pick out the school supplies she'd need for the coming year. They carefully selected folders and notebooks, discussed whether skinny or fat markers would be best, and made thoughtful decisions at each of the different tables where we had set out supplies for free distribution to all kids who came.

Though scenes like this were repeated hundreds of times that afternoon, this one stood out. That's because of what had happened during the six weeks prior.

Each Sunday since the first of the "Back to School" fliers arrived, this same woman came to church carrying a bag with a few school supplies to donate to the cause. And in the end she both gave and received about the same amount of materials.

But she didn't know how much she would receive when she stated to give. And though she really didn't have the money to both buy supplies for her own daughter and to give supplies to the drive at the church, she had enough faith to be a part of the giving and the humility to accept that which she received.

Her courage showed me how to take a solid Kingdom stance amid a "me first" world. And her simple acts of giving as blessed and receiving as a blessing reminded me of the power and the possibility that comes when generosity is a two-way street.

May I live likewise.

Thy Kingdom come on earth as it is in heaven.

ALWAYS

It had gotten dangerous.

I'd known him since he was a little kid and we'd always gotten along. I'd baptized him when he was a teen and though he'd since dropped out of church life, we visited regularly and kept up with each other's lives.

Though he ran his operation's territory on the streets with cruel, brute force, my family and I were always safe around him. He also made sure that his associates didn't mess with us, either.

But over about a six month time period, he went from friendly to cordial. Then to ambivalent. After that he started making subtle aggressive gestures toward me and toward the church.

Those gestures became less and less subtle. The family and I weren't afraid of him, but we knew not to engage him and to always give him his space.

I don't know what brought about these changes. I was not happy with them and carried a growing concern about what might be next.

So I was a little apprehensive when he stepped out of a doorway onto the sidewalk in front of me that evening. I tried to move out of his way but he blocked my path then cornered me with my back to a car.

"I got the Birthday card from the church," he said. "You all are the ones who *always* remember. Thanks." He left.

We've been fine ever since.

Finding ways of being consistent in ministry, from always having the church doors open at the scheduled times to always sending a birthday card, is an important way to show God's love. Because His love isn't dependant on the weather or the season and He's not too busy to remember to be present with us.

Clearly, I'm not God and I forget a lot of things. Plus the weather impacts what I want to do and my mood gets the best of me sometimes.

But when His followers come together as the Church and prioritize what we will *always* make sure is done, mood and weather notwithstanding, we live the love of the One who loves us, even when we're in a season when we've become simply cordial or ambivalent or worse toward Him.

For it's through His consistent love that the brute forces of the world will surrender.

Lord, thank you for promising to be with me always.

OUTLET

All our work seemed in vain once the lights went out.

Yes, it was Easter Sunday. The thousands of invitations had been distributed door-to-door and church members had been inviting friends and family to join in the celebration.

But overnight the power went out. Some people overslept because their alarm clocks were off. Others didn't have hot water to clean up with so they didn't feel presentable in public. Some got distracted by the outage and forgot that it was Sunday or lost track of time. Others figured we'd cancel the services. All these folks missed church that day.

And those were the people who attend faithfully.

Since the area of the outage roughly coincided with the area we'd done all our marketing, who knows how many others who were considering attending didn't?

So, on what is historically one of the busiest days for churches across the globe, we had but a handful of worshippers gathered in a cold, dark church.

Yet one of our electric outlets worked just fine that morning. The only place with any power for several city blocks was the socket right next to the cross. We were able to plug in our sound system and have music to sing together in our celebration of resurrection.

Despite the cold, dark, confused world around us, we found the one source of power to help us lift our voices and hearts.

I have to think of those women who, after a very confusing week, went to a cold, dark tomb. Well beyond their imagination they found the one outlet of Power in their world. In *our* world.

And though there were just a few of them, the disciples soon followed and within a couple of months there were thousands drawing from that Source.

So when my world is cold, dark, and confusing, I hope I can remember to go back to the cross seeking the power of Resurrection that will turn my voice to praise. That work is never in vain and I'll find Easter all over again.

To you, Lord, be all glory, honor, and power.

BALCONY

I would have raised an eyebrow, too, if my children came home from school telling me that their class had been to a local house of worship for activities, especially if that place's faith tradition had a reputation of doing things like burning the holy book of my faith. So I was glad when the women, clad in headscarves as a way of showing respect to God, came in with their daughters' classes.

They stayed with their daughters' groups throughout the event as we taught peacemaking skills and better ways to get along with one another as we share this planet.

As it happened, that day's staff also included many nursing students from a nearby university who were earning hours in community engagement. By their dress, it was clear to all that they were of the Jewish tradition.

So there, in a the balcony of a little church in an overlooked inner-city neighborhood, practicing Christians, Muslims, and Jews came together for a couple of hours to teach their kids how to live more at peace with one another.

I don't think what took place in the balcony of the church that day happened many other places on the planet that year. For a few minutes at least, long histories of swords, guns, bombs, and bloodshed were replaced with crayons, jigsaw puzzles, puppets, and laughter as our mutual faith-filled hope for a better world was shared together by teaching kids the ways of peace.

So I have to wonder what other seemingly obscure places peace might be being birthed for a new generation. I shouldn't be surprised, really, that hope for the world might start in such an odd place. After all, I worship a God whose incarnation began in a stable in a small town in Judea.

Thank you, Lord, for letting us witness You in ways we could not have imagined.

HOLD

Even I was hesitant about his baptism and confirmation. I'm quite generous when it comes to sharing in the sacraments and I have received lots of raised eyebrows and occasional verbal criticism over the years about it. But this one was stretching me.

This kid had only come to church once or twice before and a couple of years had passed since he'd been to one of our activities. Though his age was still noted in single digits, he had a bit of a challenged reputation throughout the community. I wasn't sure if he had any idea of what the sacraments of baptism and confirmation were about.

But he showed up carrying a towel and change of clothes that morning, as did his cousins who were scheduled to be baptized. Grandma said she'd been teaching him about Jesus and the Bible and that he was ready. With her teaching, I felt even more confident that he really *didn't* know what this was all about.

At that point, with the service ready to start, I figured that trying to explain my hesitations and requesting he wait for either of the sacraments would cause confusion and division within the family. More harm would come from *not* doing as he and his grandmother requested so a little later in the hour he was baptized and confirmed along with his cousins.

Nearly a month later I was hanging out with the guys at the local Laundromat. While visiting, one asked me if I knew, or at least knew of, this kid. When I said, "Yes," the other men started to shake their heads in frustration over him and his situation.

But then a couple of them excitedly interrupted to ask the others if they had seen this boy lately.

"Something must have happened to him a few weeks back," they noted. "It's like something got hold of him. Yeah, like something *really good* got hold of him. He's just different somehow -- and in a good way!"

They didn't know that he'd been baptized. They didn't know of the prayer confirming the Holy Spirit's presence in a new way in his life. They only knew that something really good had gotten hold of him.

I have to wonder how many times I've let my fears about what other people might think and my own self doubt become barriers to the Spirit taking hold of someone or something in my life. When did I think I was too good or too smart or too something -- anything -- to guide them to the Living Water? When did I think I was not good enough or not smart enough or not something -- anything -- to bring a confirmation of the presence of God in a situation?

My list of when the fears and doubts ruled the day dwarfs the few times I've gotten it right. But there is

One who, despite my disconnect, my cluelessness, my misinformation, and my reputation invites me into His presence. And though I never really know what He's up to, I always seem to leave having had another drink from his fountain and being blessed by his touch.

I think He still has a little hope in me. And maybe if I faithfully hold tight enough to this hope, someone, even if it's just me the midst of all my dirty laundry, will note that something Good has gotten hold of me.

Lord, let my hope be in You alone.

FREE

She stepped away from her booth during a lull in traffic and made a bee line to me. I was sitting just a few yards away registering people as they came into the church for the health fair.

Her organization had been invited by one of the university's health fair planners. Her focus was on HIV and AIDS ----- awareness, prevention, testing, counseling, and the like.

And I had noticed her work. Focused, passionate, professional, compassionate care flowed from her as she provided absolute dignity and respect in each interaction with everyone who came to her booth. She was clearly working in the center of her calling and giftedness.

So as she came up to me she said, "I want to let you know how much I appreciate this space and the atmosphere you folks at this church have created here. I set up booths in churches, community centers, schools and lots of places all over this city and this is the *only* place I go where I feel completely free to do my job. No one here is judging me or the people who come to my booth. Lots of places get squeamish with me talking about condoms or hypodermic needles and, I mean, sometimes I know people need our services but they're afraid to stop by because of what others might think. That just isn't a problem here. I'm actually free to do my job and the people who come here feel free to let me do it. I'll come back here any time you want."

I responded in kind about how much we appreciated her work, but as she left I was hit with utter shame.

Here she was working for healing and wholeness in peoples' lives. Here she was moving people toward greater righteousness. Here she was desperate to serve those who are often considered among the least in our society.

And yet day after day she only found hostile environments in which to she could operate. For that matter, she probably came to our building that afternoon *expecting* to be restricted in her service.

I hope her experience gave her some strength to carry on. I hope even more that those of us who are " . . . really and unquestionably free" (John 8:36 (AB)) will generously share that blessing.

Lord, let us be sanctuaries of life and freedom.

ROBBED

He phoned to offer me some consolation.

Word had gotten around that when we were setting up for the month's youth fellowship night we discovered some items missing. Our video game system had attached to sticky fingers and gone out the door of the church.

Again.

It's frustrating when things are stolen, especially when you're counting on using them. Not having the money to replace them makes it even worse.

So it was kind of him to call and I appreciated it.

In the conversation he was much more upset about robbery than I was. It wasn't so much that he was stuck on the fact that the thing went missing. He just couldn't get past that someone stole something from a church.

Getting worn down in his despair, I finally said, "You know, if things don't get stolen from the church once in a while then we're probably not working too hard at reaching the people who need to be here the most."

Because, oddly enough, there was real victory in the robbery. It wasn't a case of breaking and entering.

Rather, someone who didn't know how to operate under the most basic of Christian principles and ethics had actually been to church! The game's absence proved it.

I'm not saying we should be foolish by leaving the doors unlocked or by not following appropriate safety and security measures. Rather, we need to be able to look through our pain and frustration and see it as a sign that we might just be doing something right.

Really, this shouldn't be too foreign of a concept for us. After all, we have giant cross on the wall.

God, in all things we give you the glory!

HIGHLY

She went on and on for a full 45 minutes, rarely, it seemed, taking a breath. And our walking simply encouraged her to follow us up and down the streets continuing her ramblings.

The president of our denomination was in town that Sunday afternoon so we spent the time between the end of our youth activities and the start of the evening service by walking around the neighborhood. We visited with people and I pointed out different places where the impact of the ministry was showing tangible results.

She accompanied us on the whole tour. Throughout the walk she told of all the wonderful things I'd done for her, her children, her grandchildren, and the whole neighborhood. She told elaborate stories in graphic detail. Never more than a few inches away from our church's leader, he got quite an earful of how wonderful I was.

And not one syllable of it was true.

Yes, the whole congregation had invested in this family for several years and in a variety of ways: funerals, camps, emergency food assistance, hospital visits, baptisms & confirmations, baby blessings ---- the list goes on. Some family members had been active in the church and were grateful for its presence.

But the stories! They weren't even close to accurate.

That's a good thing, too, as some of what she said I did was in clear violation of the church's basic policies and, for that matter, questionably legal. It's not exactly what I want being told about me.

Still, it was her testimony and her praise without ceasing that was clearly on display that afternoon.

When the president and I finally stepped into my house she went on her way. He turned to me, smiled, and said, "Well, she certainly thinks highly of you."

Based on the previous hour, that was the day's understatement.

I so wish I was more like her. Not in the "creativity" of her stories but in her unabashed thankfulness.

God has invested a lot in me over the years in such a variety of ways: temporal, eternal, spiritual, physical -- -- more than I can even begin to recognize. Yet my praise pales in relation to who He is. His blessings are so abundant I hardly know what to even be thankful for.

Plus I'm quite certain that I've been oblivious to the

vast majority of blessings, too. My testimonies of Him probably miss the point of what He was doing more often than not and may not be exactly what He wants said about Himself to others.

I hope as I try to follow Him around I can do more than ask Him about what needs to be done or for blessings for myself and others. I hope through my praise and thanksgiving He will know that I certainly think highly of Him.

Lord, Your are worthy of all praise!

Other Books by Jeffrey Anderson

Before You Leave My House
99 Things Dad Wants You to Remember
ISBN 9781312774933

Saturday under the FreeWAY
ISBN 9781105763601

THIS WEEK at the POWER HOUSE
(Volumes 1 and 2)
ISBN 9781105166839 and 9781105178856

All titles available at lulu.com